HORSE CAPTURE FOR GLORY; HORSE THIEVERY FOR PROFIT,

OR, A SHORT HISTORY OF FLEET EQUINES IN THE AMERICAN WEST

HORSE CAPTURE FOR GLORY; HORSE THIEVERY FOR PROFIT,

OR, A SHORT HISTORY OF FLEET EQUINES IN THE AMERICAN WEST

Table of Contents

PREFACE vii

AGES AGO: INTO A NEW ERA 1

THE SPANIARDS' PRIZE 5

THE TRIBAL PRIZE 11

COUNTING COUP ON THE PIONEERS, or, TROUBLE ON THE "MEDICINE LINE" 23

THE QUEST FOR PROFIT, or, TURNING HORSE THIEVES INTO ANGELS 33

LATER . . . IN NORTH DAKOTA 53

EPILOGUE: WILD AGAIN 59

APPENDIX A. 73

APPENDIX B. 81

SOURCES OF INFORMATION 85

Preface

Early in 2015, Arnold Ceynar, at that time a casual acquaintance, called me with a proposal. He thought that his great-grandfather, a gentleman named Mac Uhlman, was worthy of induction into the North Dakota Cowboy Hall of Fame. Part of Uhlman's background was participating in cleaning out the horse-thief trade plaguing the ranchers along the Montana-North Dakota border in 1901. Arnold wondered if I would be interested in participating in the research project around these events.

The following day, a Monday, I met Arnold at the Glendive Public Library. He had a vast assortment of materials related to Mac Uhlman. He said his purpose was two-fold: he wanted to assemble information regarding his grandfather's recognition, and possibly present a historical account of the events of 1901.

The idea of researching frontier horse thievery was not an entirely new one. Over the years I have worked on several research projects with Doug Ellison, the proprietor of Western Edge Books, a fine emporium in Medora, North Dakota. Doug and I share a twisted interest in Western outlawry. Together, we mused and had desultory discussions on putting together a volume separating fact from fiction about an age-old Western crime spree. It became an opportunity that fell into my lap.

First, I did some preliminary research on newspapers.com to find out if there was anything to Arnold's story. I immediately found that there was. That piqued my interest that maybe this wasn't some more Western folklore, and that it might merit additional investigation. The idea was "hatched," and stayed where it was due to work constraints as a railroad conductor (I'm now retired).

From a historical prospective, the first challenge was how to "distill" a very wide topic (horses) into one that was quite specific (horse thievery). How can a thorough, but succinct, account be produced that would tie all the loose ends together? Where to start and where to end?

I decided to start at the beginning. I think it is important to tell the whole story, with the emergence of the horse as a large, fleet, grass-eating mammal. I don't want to get bogged down with scientific tangents—I'm not a horse biologist nor do I claim to be.

And then I think it proper to take the story into the present-day history is continuous, and we're part of it.

I don't ever claim to be an expert on anything. In the completion of this project, a few people deserve a special note of gratitude. Arnold Ceynar has a good nuts-and-bolts knowledge of ranch life. He knew that with me, born in Pennsylvania and raised in Ohio, he was dealing with somebody with limited knowledge of ranching (a "tenderfoot"). (Although I've been in Montana for almost forty years, I still consider myself somewhat of a "furriner." I have been, however, given some exposure on myriad historical projects.) Arnold told me of his biography, interesting, humble, and genuine. He and I worked together for years putting this together, sharing lots of ideas, personal reflections, and good times in the field. It is a privilege to know him.

Another note of thanks goes to my friend Lance Kalfell. Our paths first crossed at the Glendive Agri-Trade Exposition in 2008. I had a map display table there, we started to talk, and that spring I was hired to produce an operations map for his ranch. From there we went on to some writing projects which led to the creation of *Since the Days of the Buffalo: A History of Eastern Montana and the Kalfell Ranch*, released in 2013. Lance, along with his late brother Kevin, relayed the details of ranching in modern America, from animal husbandry to ranch infrastructure to government regulations to getting on with one's neighbors—a truly personal account. In the present book he brought me up to speed on government public lands policy—spoken as a participant, not as an onlooker. Most importantly, we've grown to be close personal friends, which serves to prove that we can coexist as Americans despite of our political differences. As it turns out, the two of us have plenty of shared values as well.

C. Adrian Heidenreich, Ph.D., is another friend and colleague deserving a special mention. A retired Professor of Native American Studies at Montana State University Billings, and an adopted member of the Crow Tribe, Adrian and I have worked on several meaningful projects, including a Historical Map of the Crow Nation and a map of the Hunt-Stuart Astorian Expedition of 1811-12. For the present work, I need to rely on his expertise of Native American culture, as well as his academic know-how. In his assessment of this book, he brought several important perspectives and pieces of information. The credit for emphasizing the spiritual connection between the Native culture and the horse goes to Adrian.

Dennis Tresidder, a print specialist and another long-term friend, provided pertinent input on how to make this a better book on a technical and visual basis. His advice is always appreciated, if not easy to accomplish. He's worked with me on quite a few projects, and I know that, on occasion, I have not always been the best stress reliever. But he's been patient with me, and his influence has invariably helped create a better end product—that's why he's so good at what he does.

Now a few personal notes. A project like this would be difficult without some degree of personal peace of mind. In no particular order, I'd like to thank my family—functional, accomplished, and contented—for their continued moral support. I'm truly grateful. Cheryl Yaskoff Martinez, my long-term, long-distance, long-suffering girlfriend, provides the emotional fuel to help me "keep-on-keepin'-on." Elizabeth Drews, who helped me recover from a serious illness and who added some constructive criticism on this project, deserves special thanks. Other friends, a few whom I have mentioned, and a few more, are truly a spice of life.

And a moment of "dime store philosophy." I've come to believe that everyone who crosses my path is confirmation of Divine Intervention.

As a final note, while all of those mentioned above, and probably not a few inadvertently omitted, provided the necessary support, this book is my responsibility, and any errors or omissions are mine alone.

(Mac Uhlman was inducted into the North Dakota Cowboy Hall of Fame in 2021.)

M.D.B. June 2021.

AGES AGO: INTO A NEW ERA

At the onset of the Cenozoic Era, sixty-five million years ago, the Earth had a much different appearance. The Earth, warmer than it is now, had vast forests, and its open spaces were filled with primitive flowering plants and scattered woodlands. Bamboo and rice were the antecedents to grasses. Palms, another type of primordial grass, appeared in the tropics of the early Tertiary Period, the initial division of the Cenozoic. Cacti evolved to occupy drier areas.

It is believed that a large comet or asteroid slammed into the present-day Yucatan Peninsula—a single, cataclysmic event at the end of the preceding Cretaceous Period (the "Age of Reptiles," which ran for approximately 80 million years from 145 to 65 million years ago) that led to the extinction of the dinosaurs, the largest reptiles. Some reptiles survived: for an unkown reason, alligators, turtles, lizards, and amphibians continued on their evolutionary paths. Many ocean organisms, mostly living near the surface, were also victims of the abrupt change in climate. Many forest plants also disappeared, but new species emerged as the atmosphere cleared for photosynthesis. Birds, thought to be descendants of the dinosaurs, were already established, and managed to survive—as did mammals, mostly the size of rodents, which were beginning their ascent to the top of the biological heap.

The Earth itself was different. The continents had a different alignment. Europe, North America, and Asia were connected; the Atlantic Ocean was just beginning to open up. To the south, South America and Antarctica were connected, and the Indian subcontinent was in its initial stages of its migration from Antarctica to Asia. The collision would result in the Himalaya Mountains.

In the Eocene epoch, about 52 million years ago, mammalian species were rapidly diversifying. The "apex species" of large reptiles were gone, leaving a biological void. There was plenty of room for mammals to grow.

One of these was the *eohippus,* the "Dawn Horse." Thought to be the size of a fox, it was a small herbiferous creature with five-toed feet, occupying both forests and open land in North America. It didn't much resemble a modern horse in appearance or habit, but it was the base of a vast family tree. A few branches survive; an unknown number of others became extinct.

About 40 million years ago, in the Oligocene epoch, modern grasses—hardy species well adapted to a more open, arid environment—began to appear. New horse species appeared, among them the *mesohippus,* about two feet tall and weighing about a hundred pounds. Its feet each had three toes, the middle toe being a primordial hoof. *Mesohippus* was both a browsing and grazing animal consuming both fruits and early grasses.

The next major link in the evolutionary chain was the *meryhippus,* dating from the Middle Miocene epoch, about 17-19 million years (m.y.) ago. *Meryhippus* was more massive than its predecessors, weighing about 200 pounds, and resembled the modern horse. Only the middle toe, the hoof, touched the ground. Its teeth became adapted for grazing prairie grasses. Lean and fleet afoot, it could outrun predators on the open plains. It was about this time that these ancestral horses are thought to have migrated from North America to Asia and Europe.

It is believed by some scientists that the following precursor was the *pliohippus,* which developed about 12 million years ago. It was a large animal, some weighing in excess of a thousand pounds. Fossil remains are widely dispersed across North America.

Equus, the modern horse, is thought to have descended from previous *genii* about four million years ago, and quickly spread from North America into Asia and Europe, as well as into South America. There are several species of *equus* worldwide, comprising horses, asses, and zebras.

As *equus* occupied an ever-increasing area, the ancestors of human beings began to emerge in East Africa. As with horses, human evolution is fraught with controversy, with many fits, starts, missing links, and dead ends. However it is widely believed that ancestral humans migrated from Africa to Europe and Asia.

During the last Ice Age, which ended about 12,000 years ago, humans are thought to have passed over the Bering Land Bridge from Siberia into North America. Some humans probably migrated by boat, arriving on the west coast. (There may have been human travelers even earlier than that, preceding the newcomers by possibly thousands of years.) The newly arrived humans quickly dispersed and possibly coincidentally, the large mammal species of North America began to become extinct: the wooly mammoth, mastodon, ancient buffalo, and the horse were likely hunted out, as well as succumbing to changes in the natural environment.

Horses are strong, proud, sociable, and adapt well to humans. Given humans' cunning, patience, management skills, and tool-making abilities, it seems inevitable that a bond would be forged with these wonderful animals.

About 6,000 years ago, humans are thought to have begun using horses for something other than a food source. Archeological evidence indicates that the Botai tribesmen of northern Kazakhstan were the first to domesticate horses, but it was perhaps also contemporaneous with cultures in Ukraine, as well as north of the Black Sea. Wild horses were also concentrated in open areas of the Iberian Peninsula, which also points to early domestication. In short order, domestic horses were present throughout Europe and Asia. Horses are believed to have reached Africa about 4,000 years ago.

Central Asian tribesmen are believed to have corralled horses for use in hunting parties. The concept of using horses as beasts of burden seems to have come at about the same time. Agricultural uses of horses caught on quickly; most evidence for early agricultural horse use was found in Eastern Europe. Within a short period of time, horses were used in warfare, which possibly accounted for the demise of the early agricultural settlements in Europe. The chariot was believed to have been invented about 4,000 years ago southeast of the Ural Mountains, and soon was utilized far and wide.

By the Dark Ages, about from 500 to 1000 C.E. (Common Era, synonymous with A.D.), horses were everywhere in the Eastern Hemisphere. It was only a matter of time before they caught a ride on a ship bound for the "New World."

The Wadsworth Dispatch.

WADSWORTH, WASHOE COUNTY, NEVADA, WEDNSDAY, AUGUST 18, 1897.

WEDNESDAY.....AUGUST 18, 1897

Origin of the Horse.

Dr. Lydekker, the English naturalist, says that while the ordinary European breeds of horses may have been derived from those which were first subjugated by the stone implement makers of western Europe, unnumbered centuries ago, it is probable that "thoroughbred" horses are of eastern origin. He thinks that Turkestan was their original home, and that the ancient Turcomans and Mongols were the first Asiatic tribes to make the wild horse the servant and friend of man. Horses, believed by some authorities to belong to a truly wild race—that is to say, whose ancestors were never domesticated—still inhabit the central Asian steppes. From Turkestan, according to Dr. Lydekker, they spread to Hindustan, Persia, Assyria, Egypt and Arabia. In the last named country they became so indispensable that many have supposed Arabia to be the original home of the horse. The interesting fact is pointed out that our North American Indians, to whom the horse was unknown before the advent of white men, have shown the same skill and adaptability in mastering them that the Arabs exhibited, so that, as Dr. Lydekker remarks, "Had we not historic evidence to the contrary there is no saying but that the original subjugation of the horse might have been attributed to the Indian of the prairies."

1897 article from wild horse country reflecting the scientific understanding of the time.

THE SPANIARDS' PRIZE 2

The year 1492 was a momentous one in Spain, marking the beginning of a sequence of events that would impact cultures around the globe: the expulsion of the Moors; the onset of the Inquisition; the voyage of a master mariner and his crew in a small fleet setting sail from Seville; and the reintroduction of horses to the Western Hemisphere.

Horses were reintroduced to the "New World" on Christopher Columbus' second voyage in 1493. These were Andalusians, bred for millennia on the Iberian Peninsula. About fifteen hands (60 inches) high at the withers (base of the neck), stallions weigh on the average 1,100 lbs., while mares weigh in at 900 lbs. Strong, compact, and well-built, they were ideal for use in warfare, and had been noted as such since the days of the ancient Greeks. The Spaniards would test their mettle.

Columbus' 1493 voyage was a three-year epic endeavor that firmly established a Spanish presence in the Caribbean Sea. Santo Domingo was settled in 1496 and soon became an administrative capital. From there, Diego Velázquez de Cuéllar brutally overran Cuba in 1511, and eventually established Havana in 1515 as a jumping-off point for the mainland of North America and as a depot for goods passing to and from what was considered the end of the Earth.

Ponce de Léon, embarking from Puerto Rico in 1513, sailed to the mainland to establish his personal empire. Exploring the coast of the Florida Peninsula, he sailed home with the idea of returning. This he did in 1521 with a force of 200 men and 50 horses, only to be greeted by hostile Colusa Natives. He died shortly after his arrival, infected by a poisoned arrow near the present site of Charlotte Harbor. (His quest for the "Fountain of Youth" was a legend that was promulgated later.)

In 1519, Hernán Cortés (full name: Hernán Cortés de Monroy y Pizzaro Altamirano), a political enemy of Velázquez de Cuéllar, landed in Mexico with about 500 men, 13 horses, and a small artillery. Cortés was the first to use the Spanish method of conquest on a large scale: overawe the Natives (in this case, the Aztecs) with their firearms, iron goods, and horses; foment tribal intrigue; capture their chieftain (Moctezuma); hold him for a king's ransom; kill him anyway; and exploit the now-leaderless tribe, leading to their subjugation. Any resistance (and there was some) was brutally suppressed, and in 1521 Cortés became governor of Mexico.

Pánfilo de Narváez, a savage veteran of the Aztec campaign (and a rival of Cortés), landed on June 27, 1527, in Tampa Bay. Seeking gold, he faced opposition from the Apalachee Indians, whereupon he arrogantly separated from his lieutenant, the able Álvar Núñez Cabeza de Vaca. De Narváez and his men built rafts to sail home and were never seen again.

Cabeza de Vaca (translated "head of a cow" for a medieval incident in Spain) and eighty men floated on their rafts and were marooned near Galveston Bay. In an epic tale of survival, the dwindling party began a seven-year transverse across Texas and northern Mexico. De Vaca, initially enslaved but

1892 Florida newspaper masthead showing Spanish explorers and the contrast between centuries.

adapting the ways of the Natives, came to be regarded as a shaman and healer. He was one of the last four survivors of the de Narváez expedition that returned to Mexico City in 1534.

The aborted de Narváez expedition nevertheless paved the way for the epic journey of Hernando de Soto (lately returned from Pizarro's conquest of the Incas) which began in 1539. Accompanied by a large retinue of 620 men (some with families), priests, artisans, farmers, merchants, and Native subjects, along with 220 horses and various other livestock, an entire village really, the party landed south of Tampa Bay. He was obviously looking for a good place to settle, ideally to establish a village near fabulous gold mines that could be worked with slave labor, with the wherewithal to be occupied and sustained long-term. In the alligator swamps of Florida, he established decent relations with the Apalachees who had so bedeviled de Narváez. However, there were not enough provisions to go around, and, starving, they ate many of their horses in today's Panhandle. The following spring, they heard rumors of gold and continued their quest northward into the woods of Georgia and the Carolinas (where there is in fact some gold). Then, De Soto and his troop explored the forests of the Appalachian Mountains, possibly as far north as present-day Knoxville, Tennessee. Venturing to the southwest, the De Soto Expedition passed into Alabama, where they hoped to reach the Gulf of Mexico for supplies. However, they encountered the hostile Coosa chief Tuskaloosa at the village of Mabila on the Alabama River. Mabila was burned, but the battle was essentially a draw. Suffering great losses, De Soto and the remainder of his men veered northward; some new evidence suggests that he crossed the Ohio River into Indiana and explored the Wabash River valley. Venturing westward, he crossed the Mississippi River in southern Illinois (some say at Memphis, Tennessee), and passed through the prairies of Missouri into Arkansas, then explored the Ouachita River valley in Arkansas and Louisiana. (The April 19, 1935 edition of the *Amarillo Globe* noted the possible site of one of De Soto's massacres near Mangham, La.) In declining health, the exhausted De Soto entered the backwater along the Mississippi River, where he expired near Lake Village, Arkansas, or Vidalia, Louisiana, on May 21, 1542. His body was filled with stones and buried in the river. The remaining party, bewildered, dejected, and surrounded by hostile Natives, escaped westward into present-day northeastern Texas. But, finding no succor, they backtracked to the Mississippi and built boats to sail toward Mexico, where they landed later that summer.

(As can be gathered from the narrative, De Soto's route is largely speculative. In 1936, a group of scholars were commissioned to pinpoint the route. With subsequent advancements in mapping, archaeology, and satellite technology, that route has been significantly modified. Still, many questions remain as to the exact path of the thousand-mile journey.)

In 1539, the Spaniards began to enter the area that was to be the American Southwest. Hearing rumors of the fabulous "Seven Cities of Cibola," Friar Marcos de Niza, another priest, and a Moorish servant, "Estevan the Black," along with a few adventurers and subjects, set out from Culiacán and crossed into what is now Arizona. Possibly passing the ruins of the abandoned Native settlement of Chichilticale (Aztec for "Red House"), the party entered a barren wilderness, and trekked northward toward the rumored "Seven Cities of Cibola." Estevan, scouting ahead, ignored orders from the Zuni chieftain not to approach Cibola and was murdered for his efforts. De Niza met the wounded remains of Estevan's small party and, alarmed, retreated to Mexico.

Having read (and misconstrued) De Niza's report, Francisco Vázquez de Coronado, the governor of Nueva Galicia in Mexico, was overcome with "gold fever." He immediately set about gathering a large expedition for the north, financed by himself. Assembling an army of 300 soldiers, mounted and unmounted, a thousand vassals, 1,200 horses, and De Niza himself, Coronado left Culiacán on April 22, 1540. About the same time, a supply party was to sail up the Colorado River. Following in De Niza's footsteps, noting the deserted Chichilticale, the impatient Coronado and a small portion of his expedition began the 15-day journey across the wasteland. Coronado battled his way into the village of Hawikuh, in the Zuni homeland. Moving to the east, it was learned that Cibola was really part of a complex of agricultural pueblos bereft of gold. (De Niza was awarded the sobriquet "the Lying Monk," even though his 1539 account mentioned no gold.)

From Hawikuh, Coronado sent a party, led by Garcia Lopez de Cárdenas, toward the rumored location of the Colorado River, hoping to obtain his supplies. Passing through the Hopi villages in northern Arizona, when they reached the Grand Canyon they found that the supplies could not be recovered in the inhospitable terrain. (The supply party, under Hernando de Alarcón, journeyed up the Colorado as far as present-day Yuma, Arizona. When they didn't find Coronado, they buried the supplies and sailed back to Mexico in their decaying boats.)

While in Cibola, Coronado heard tales of untold wealth far to the east, at a fabled settlement called Quivera. Never one to discount a rumor, he and his reunited party moved eastward. They passed Acoma pueblo (now noted as the oldest continuously inhabited community in the United States) and entered the Rio Grande valley in the vicinity of Albuquerque. There, facing resistance, they massacred hundreds of Tiguex Natives and destroyed their pueblos. There they spent the winter and prepared for a long journey to the east.

Guided by a Native they called "the Turk," Coronado's party set out for Quivera in the spring of 1541. The first obstacle was the Llano Estacado ("Staked Plains"), a vast, flat, treeless prairie stretching for 150 miles into the Texas Panhandle. Leaving archaeological evidence near Floydada, Texas, the expedition turned to the northeast. Marching over 300 miles over open country, following rumors and hearsay, they came to a substantial agricultural settlement north of the Arkansas River near present-day Lyons, Kansas, inhabited by ancestors of the Wichita Indians. There was no gold to be found there, only agricultural treasure: corn, squash, and beans. "The Turk," part of the expedition for hundreds of miles, was executed for allegedly misleading the *conquistador*. Coronado's entourage beat a hasty retreat and wintered in the pueblo country near Albuquerque, returning to Mexico in the summer of 1542. Although it covered thousands of miles of uncharted terrain, Coronado's quest for plunder was an abject failure.

After the dismal Coronado expedition, the Spaniards did not return to New Mexico for almost 40 years. In 1581, a small group of clergy, soldiers, and subjects, organized by Friar Agustin Rodríguez and led by a gentleman dubbed "El Chamuscado" (Spanish for "scorched" because of his flaming red beard), followed the Rio Grande northward in search of Native souls to convert to Christianity, a thought never far from a *conquistador's* mind. Venturing up as far as the pueblos near Socorro, New Mexico, one friar decided to return to Mexico and was murdered soon after his departure. The party marched eastward to the Pecos River valley, where they found more Native villages populated by buffalo hunters. The explorers wintered near the Zuni villages, and the following spring the soldiers returned to Mexico, leaving behind the clergy to continue their work.

Antonio De Espejo arrived from Spain in 1571, along with a priest named Pedro Moya de Contreras who was tasked with bringing the Inquisition to Mexico. By 1582, Espejo was well established as a rancher in Chihuahua, but was on the run from the Spanish authorities, accused of murder. In November of that year, he organized an expedition of himself, a priest, 30 subjects, and 115 horses, to learn the whereabouts of the two priests left behind by the Rodríguez party the year before, and to examine the possibility of establishing a Spanish colony in New Mexico. Working their way down the Conchos River and thence up the Rio Grande, they arrived at the Pueblo villages in February of 1583. There they learned that the priests had been murdered after Rodríguez's departure. Seeking rumored silver deposits in present-day Arizona, they passed through the Zuni and Hopi settlements, but were disappointed with the results—where, ironically, in the early 1900s, would be the fabulous copper camp of Jerome, Arizona. At the supposed mines, the party split up, some returning to Mexico. On the way, they had a skirmish at Acoma pueblo. The rest of the troop returned to Mexico by way of the Pecos River, arriving home in September of 1583. In the process, they received credit as the first Europeans to extensively explore what was then referred to as the "*Rio de las Vacas*" for the extensive bison herds along the route.

About 1594 (the date is uncertain), a small party, consisting of Antonio Gutierrez de Umana, Francisco de Leyba, Jusepe (a Native guide), along with soldiers and subjects, left Culiacán on an illegal expedition to New Mexico. After wintering in the Rio Grande pueblos, they set out across the Plains to the "Great Settlement" (maybe Quivera), which most likely was along the Arkansas River. Continuing toward the northeast, Umana and Leyba got into a dispute whereupon Leyba was stabbed to death. Farther on, the group may have sighted a big river (the Missouri?). Not far from there, Jusepe and five Indians departed the fractured party. Jusepe was captured by the Natives (rumored to be Apaches); the others were killed. After spending a year with his captors, Jusepe was able to return to Mexico. The rest of the party was never seen again, possibly massacred in northeastern Kansas.

After over a half-century of desultory exploration, in 1595 the King Philip II of Spain decreed that New Mexico be colonized. To this end he assigned Juan de Oñate, son of a wealthy Zacatecas mine owner. Oñate was Spain's ideal of a conqueror: well-heeled, well-bred (he was a direct descendant of both Cortés and Moctezuma), courageous, and filled with religious zeal. Setting out northward from Zacatecas in the spring of 1598, Oñate, along with a party of 400 colonists (some with families), no doubt many vassals, 83 wheeled vehicles (foreign to the Natives in the "New World"), and *seven thousand* head of livestock, they slowly crossed sandy deserts of Chihuahua. Shortly after reaching the Rio Grande at present-day El Paso, Texas, on April 30 Oñate declared New Mexico to be under the dominion of Spain. Proceeding up the Rio Grande, he established his capital at San Juan be Las Caballos, near Taos. Leaving his slow-moving cavalcade, Oñate led a vanguard to explore the upper reaches of the Canadian River. Reversing course, they reached the Acoma Pueblo, where the Natives refused to supply the Oñate troop with provisions that they needed for themselves, and in the ensuing skirmish killed eleven Spaniards. Continuing westward, they spent the winter at the Zuni Pueblos. Leaving Zuni in January of 1599, the small army exacted a terrible retribution against the Natives at Acoma Pueblo, slaughtering as many as a thousand in what was to become known as the Acoma Massacre. The remainder were enslaved; men over 25 had a foot amputated.

After the brutal introduction, Oñate returned to San Juan, from where, in 1601, he, along with 130 soldiers, a dozen priests, 350 horses and mules, and numerous ox-carts, set out toward the fabled city of Quivera, the idea that would not die. Following the Canadian River into present-day Oklahoma, they found the Native settlements in today's central Kansas, where they were the latest to be disappointed.

Returning to New Mexico, they found that the colony had foundered, in no small part due to the harsh treatment of the Natives. Oñate, ever the explorer, left the increasingly desperate colony in 1604, and explored the lower Colorado River to the Gulf of California, returning to New Mexico in the winter of 1605.

Meanwhile, word got back to Spain of Oñate's brutality (even by Spanish standards) toward the pueblo Natives. In 1606, he was recalled to Mexico City for an inquiry, and was removed as governor in 1607. The wheels of justice turned slowly, and in 1613, Oñate was forever banished from New Mexico, and exiled to Spain for five years. He never returned, and died in Spain in 1626.

Oñate's successor as governor, Pedro de Peralta, facing Native attacks in San Juan, moved the capital to the new, more defensible settlement of Santa Fe in 1610, and a new regime was introduced to New Mexico.

Subsequent to conquest, the Spaniards introduced the *encomienda* system to rule over the indigenous peoples. Somewhat akin to feudalism, the *encomienda* was a grant of Native labor bestowed to individuals deemed worthy by the Spanish crown, the land retained by the royalty. The Natives were to be provided subsistence, protection, and religious training in Christianity. In return, the Natives were expected to provide tribute in the form of crops or treasure to the *encomienderos*, or grant holders. While Queen Isabella banned outright slavery in the "New World," this was, in fact, *de facto* enslavement, and the Natives suffered untold hardships and cruelty under the *encomienda*.

The system did not prosper in New Mexico. The Natives, who had scraped out a livelihood through feast and famine for centuries, were resistant to subjugation. The Spanish invaders regarded the Natives as vassals, a disposable source of labor whose souls yearned for conversion. In addition, by the 1650s an intense rivalry emerged between Franciscan priests and the secular colonists, dividing Spanish leadership, and their ambitions.

A few watershed events in the Spanish northern colony signaled the harbinger of revolt. In about 1656, Fray Alonso de Poseta, a Franciscan missionary, brought the full force of the Inquisition to New Mexico. It was decreed that the Natives abandon their beliefs and destroy their religious symbols. In 1675, forty-seven Native shamans were brought before a court of Inquisition in Santa Fe—four were hanged, and the remainder were lashed and imprisoned. After rumors of Native unrest, the Spanish governor set them free. Additionally, the 1670s were a time of intense drought and famine in the desert, adding to the misery of both the enslaved and their captors.

After the 1675 Inquisition, a charismatic leader known as Popé emerged for the Pueblo Natives. Thought to have been born about 1630 in San Juan Pueblo, the rest of Popé's early life seems to have been lost to antiquity. For several years in the late 1670s, he united the far-flung Pueblo villages to throw off the Spanish yoke.

The Pueblo Revolt was scheduled to begin on August 11, 1680. Amid concerns of secrecy, Popé began the insurrection a day early. The Natives isolated Santa Fé, home to about 2,400; about 400 colonists perished "at the edge of the sword." Within three days the Spaniards were driven southward, and shortly thereafter abandoned New Mexico for El Paso. The colonists were expelled until 1692, until the "Reconquest," but even after that, the foreign dominion was considerably weakened.

By 1680, the Spanish colonists possessed thousands of horses, which the Natives had been forbidden to own outright. The horses were promptly captured by the Native insurrectionists, beginning the equine migration toward the northern Great Plains. One event, the Pueblo Rebellion, would revolutionize a manner of living among tribal nations scattered over a million square miles.

THE TRIBAL PRIZE 3

The Pueblo culture is one of the oldest on Earth, traceable for over seven millennia. At the time of the Spanish conquest, they led a vibrant and sustainable way of life consisting of small-scale horticulture, hunting native deer and antelope, and trading among tribes. Additionally, their pottery skills were recognized far and wide.

Also present were the Apaches, an Athabaskan tribe whose origins were far to the northwest, in present-day Oregon, Washington, and British Columbia. They were proximate to the Pueblos for centuries, possibly as far back as 1000 C.E. While the reason for their long migration is unclear, a rumor is that they had a falling-out with their tribal brethren long ago. The Apache were big-game hunters—a mainstay of their diet was the American bison. More warlike than their neighbors, they subjected the Pueblos to constant harassment. The Pueblo villages were caught in a vise between Spanish oppression and Apache raids.

To the east, in territory explored by Coronado, were various tribes of Caddoan descent, which originated in the Lower Red River valley in the swamps and canebrakes of northern Louisiana. The Ouachita tribe, a mound-building culture, migrated northwestward to the Arkansas River valley long before the Spanish exploration, and became known as the Wichitas. The Pawnee tribe, descendants of the Wichitas, continued the northward journey, to the lower Platte River valley in present-day Nebraska. All these tribes were horticultural, seasonally hunting buffalo.

At the time of the Pueblo Rebellion, the Natives were not unfamiliar with horses. The Spaniards, while forbidding their Native subjects direct ownership of horses, oversaw their use in the tasks assigned to their vassals: farming, freighting, mining, and road-building. Over decades the Pueblos were well aware of how these beasts of burden could be utilized.

After defeating the Spaniards in the Rebellion, the Pueblos were immediately mobilized. They could continue to farm without the back-breaking labor, and participate in their far-flung trading network in greater volume. Shortly, horses were in the hands of the Utes, allies to the Pueblos, a Shoshonean-speaking tribe in the Four Corners tablelands to the northwest.

In the meantime, the Apaches, who were reported to possess small groups of horses as early as 1623, were quick to capture large herds of Spanish horses that could be used to hunt buffalo and wage war. They were to become the terror of the Southwestern Plains for the next two centuries.

To the Natives, horses became more than tools which made work easier. A spiritual bond quickly came to exist between Native Americans and their recent acquisitions.

Symbolic names were applied to horses: "big dog," "spirit dog," "spirit elk"; the Apsaalooke (Crow) name for "horse" is *iichiile,* related to the word for elk, *iichiikaashe,* or "real horse."

Fanciful Native images from the 1850s.

The alliance between human and horse was visceral. A horse was found to run faster, see farther, carry more, and cover terrain better than humans. At the same time, horses could be trained to perform necessary tasks and tricks. A durable animal, servile yet independent, filled the bill for the ascendency of tribal culture. Humans were "the brains of the operation," and their newfound possession was considered a worthy confederate.

To declare that the horse revolutionized the tribal way of life is a question of semantics. There is no doubt that horses accelerated tribal development and ultimately, demise. Horses enabled tribal members to perform age-old tasks, such as hunting and migration, more efficiently—a horse could carry a payload about four times that of the dogs used previously—but basic survival techniques changed very gradually. (However, the use of dogs as beasts of burden was never entirely abandoned.) At the same time, the Great Plains tribal ranges expanded exponentially. Before the arrival of the horses the tribal range could be counted in tens of miles; afterward, Natives could venture hundreds.

By 1700, the steady, inexorable horse dispersion was well underway. Via the "Moccasin Telegraph" (the intertribal rumor mill) news spread far northwest to the Upper Platte valley in Wyoming. A large band of the Arapaho tribe migrated to the southern plains, and became the Comanche tribe. It may be argued that they relocated directly because of the availability of horses. In short order, certainly within a generation, they became expert equestrians.

Dispersal of the horse followed four principal routes: eastward through Texas toward the Red River valley; northeastward through present-day Oklahoma, Kansas, Nebraska and into Wyoming, eastern Montana and finally the Canadian prairies; northwestward over the west slope of the Rockies to Idaho, Oregon, Washington, and back over the Rockies to the Flathead and Blackfeet tribes in Montana and Alberta; and westward into California.

The process took some time. Horses were traded between friends and captured by foes. It is believed that the Pawnees in present-day Nebraska had horses by 1720; the Crows in southcentral and eastern Montana by 1725; the Blackfeet along the northern Rocky Mountain Front by about 1750; and lastly the Canadian Crees of the far-northern Great Plains about 1770. During this time, the tribes, one after another, became experts in horsemanship. The Nez Perce in Idaho and Oregon extensively bred their horses into prized appaloosas.

There are a few extant reports of the initial reaction as horses were introduced. James H. Bradley, a U.S. Army officer, recalled the following oral account from Little Face, a Crow scout:

> "... [his grandfather remembered] at that time [about 1730] the Crows had no horses ... At last, after they had reached they reached the Yellowstone country ... they were visited by a party of Nez Perces [from present-day Idaho and Oregon], and saw that they used only dogs and told them of the larger and better animals possessed by themselves and offered to trade them some if they would visit their camp. A party of Crows did so ..."

A differing account holds that the Crows obtained their horses from the Comanches of Texas. As the Comanches were a branch of the Arapahoes of Wyoming and the Crow Nation was a trading hub, that arrangement also seems feasible. It may also be that the Crows used *both* tribes as sources of their horses.

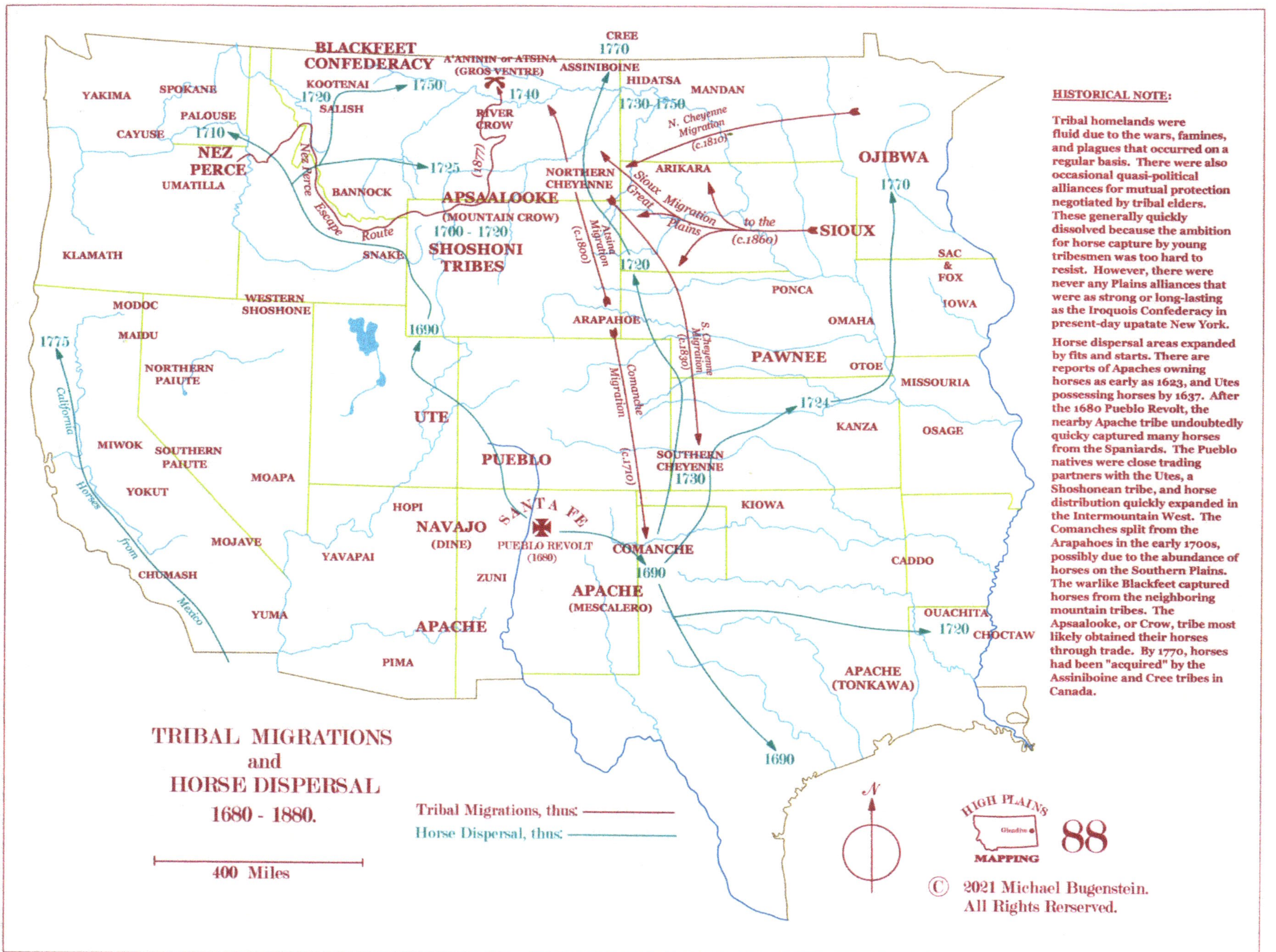

Tribal dispersals and horse migrations, 1680–1880.

Horses, with their ability to quickly cover wide distances, were useful primarily on the open lands of the American West and Great Plains. In the Eastern woodlands, horses were of questionable value, and actually impeded silent movement in times of war.

The tribes tended their horses like the assets they were. Accumulated into large herds, horses were regarded as sources of work, prowess, and prestige. A typical Crow village may have possessed a herd of over a thousand. These were mostly work horses used to carry the village to a distant camp or the products of a hunt. Young boys were generally given the responsibility for tending the animals that were left to graze; horses, being social animals, tended not to wander too far. Prized war horses or those specialized for hunting, often marked with dyed symbols or hand prints, were likely picketed close to their master's lodge. A length of sinew was used to alert a sleeping Native that his horse was being disturbed—sometimes bells or shells, acquired through trade, would also be used as an alarm.

As the young herders matured, they would learn horsemanship from the older warriors who would teach their techniques. By the time a young tribesman was in his mid-teens, he was likely to be a skilled horseman. Often older girls, likewise eager to learn, would mature into artful *equestriennes.*

The tribal method of hunting bison did not change for generations: buffalo were surrounded and impounded in enclosures and slaughtered with arrows or driven off cliffs and, being stunned, were then dispatched. In the olden days, dogs were used to herd buffalo; horses, being larger, swifter, and more mobile, greatly expedited the process. The womenfolk were then expected to butcher the animals, dress and cure the meat, and tan the hides for clothes and lodges. Horses somewhat eased the burden on women carrying the products of the hunt.

Warfare, a common denominator in cultures worldwide, had been practiced by the Natives since time immemorial. While traditionally the concept of individual land ownership was foreign to the tribes, the notion of territorial possession and demanding tribute was not. Tribal strategists would plan their attacks for quick, stealthy strikes with a minimum of casualties. Warlike tribes would subjugate, and sometimes annihilate, their more peaceful brethren, such as the infamous liquidation of the Illinois tribe by the Iroquois in the late 1670s (accomplished without horses). Warfare was also utilized for the capture of hostages: men were tested for their courage (often under torture), while women and children were likely to be adopted into the tribe; in this way, population loss due to disease, famine, or warfare could be replaced. By acquiring horses, all these facets of warfare were vastly broadened.

At about the same time, firearms were slowly introduced by the European traders just beginning to infiltrate the Great Plains. At first, the tribes regarded guns as slow and unwieldy, but within a generation or two became widely accepted as adjuncts to the bow and arrow and the lance.

In war, many tribes practiced a gamesmanship called "counting coup." The premise was attaining glory through daring deeds. The most coveted coup was snatching an enemy's gun in battle. Also high on the list was taking an enemy's wife. Killing an adversary carried less prestige—that would effectively, and permanently, end a game that was supposed to be ongoing. Counting coup was essentially outsmarting an enemy; deception was considered praiseworthy.

Tribal life was not without diversion. Games involving skill and athleticism had always been a pastime. The arrival of horses brought new sources of entertainment. Horse racing became a passion for tribal members, as well as other forms of skilled horsemanship. As various neighboring tribes acquired horses, another pursuit was soon underway.

The Plains tribes quickly discovered capturing enemy horses as a new path to glory. As the value of horses became evident members of one tribe began capturing the horses from another, beginning a colorful quest that became a Great Plains legend.

Ba-da-ah-chon-du (He Who Outjumps All), a Crow Chief on Horseback, by George Catlin (c.1836).

Horse capture became a war objective in and of itself. The accomplishment took on several important meanings. Horses quickly became a measure of wealth as well as a medium of exchange. Capturing horses helped young tribesmen become expert warriors, honing survival skills for himself and for the tribe as a whole. A young warrior who could capture many horses could be considered a good provider for a potential mate. And, not the least, the glory of counting coups would help a young man rise in tribal stature and leadership.

A tribal horse raid was a stealthy, meticulously-planned operation. The typical raid consisted of a war party, small enough to travel quickly and quietly, large enough to defend itself, generally consisting of about ten reliable tribesmen: a few young warriors, two or three "braves" coming of age, and a seasoned veteran as a leader. After quiet planning and packing lightly (spare moccasins, a bow and arrow or light firearm, lengths of rope sinew, and a bag of "strong medicine" to ensure protection and good fortune, all wrapped in a light pelt) the war party set out, on foot, on a journey that might cover six hundred miles. At the outset, the raiders, the Blackfeet perhaps (located along the present-day Canadian border), travelled during the day, but after entering enemy territory (maybe occupied by the Crows, in present-day southern Montana and northern Wyoming) they moved at night. As they neared an enemy village, the war party built a war lodge as a base of operations, preparation, and reconnaissance.

Snake Indian Pursuing a "Crow" Horse Thief, by Alfred Jacob Miller (c.1840).

After the enemy village was located, the actual raid was carefully crafted. The village would be "surveyed" to locate the lodges, where prized horses were tethered and where the main horse herd was corralled. After prayers and appeals for "good medicine" the war party was ready for its raid.

Near sunrise, the Crows' village would be quietly entered. The enemy, hopefully still asleep, would be unaware of the incursion. The raiders would mollify barking dogs with bits of meat carried for the purpose. Horses tied near the Crow lodges would be captured in silence. Then the horses in the main herd were selectively led away. The raiders then make their escape, leaving as quietly as they came, generally with a few dozen horses that could be herded vast distances.

At least that was the plan. The Crows were ever-vigilant to such an occurrence, and could not be counted on to slumber while their main source of wealth and transportation was being plundered. More often than not, the Crow would instantly arise armed for battle. After an initial salvo of arrows and rifle fire, a chase would be on across the plains, the Blackfeet holding onto the best horses and the Crows trying to recover their losses. There was a likelihood of casualties on both sides, giving the battle a new urgency. If any raiders survived, they headed for home, mounted. After the Blackfeet warriors reached their home lodges, possibly hundreds of miles away, a celebration was held for their successful raid and the booty distributed to those deemed worthy. Vows for revenge for fallen comrades would be uttered. Tribesmen had long memories.

If the Crow successfully repelled the raid and took enemy casualties, they held a macabre celebration of their victory, and waited for the inevitable retribution. And so the cycle continued.

(The foregoing account was written by John C. Ewers in his seminal book *The Blackfeet: Raiders on the Northwestern Plains,* and based on Blackfeet oral tradition.)

Of course the Blackfeet and the Crow were not the only ones participating in this ritual. All the plains tribes, from the Cree in the north to the Comanche in the south, raided their neighbors near and far for equine plunder. On the Great Plains, at that time totally a tribal domain, some tribes would thus demonstrate their ascendency, and some their regression. It was truly survival of the fittest.

In the late 1860s, the United States Army, victorious in the War Between the States, turned its attention to "pacifying" the Natives on the Great Plains. Most of the action took place along the Bozeman Trail, which ran from Fort Laramie on the North Platte River, across the rich Wyoming grasslands, home to the buffalo, thence around the Big Horn Mountains, finally following the Yellowstone River toward the Gallatin Valley in Montana. It was a dangerous path for the pioneers—the Oglala Sioux and Northern Cheyenne tribes jealously protected their prized buffalo hunting ground. Finally, the U.S. Army, after major losses in a three-year war with the tribes, abandoned their forts and closed the Bozeman Trail to passage.

Another major tribal area of operations was a vast, porous common hunting ground north of the Marias and Missouri rivers in Montana Territory. A tribal reserve, ostensibly set aside for the Piegan, Blood, Blackfeet, Atsina (Gros Ventre of the Prairie), and River Crow Tribes. The United States Government established several trading posts: the Old Agency and Piegan Agency near the Rocky Mountain Front; Fort Browning, a Gros Ventre agency, near present-day Dodson, Montana (soon abandoned and burnt); the Milk River Post, near Chinook; and agencies at Fort Peck and Poplar River in northeastern Montana. A few pioneers and gold seekers, perhaps with a greater sense of adventure (or greed) than good judgement, located on the prairie around that time.

By the early 1880s, the 40,000+ square mile northern tribal reserve, due to the addition of dislocated Natives from the Indian Wars in southern Montana, relocated warlike Sioux tribes from the east, Canadian Cree buffalo hunters, and under pressure from impatient white settlers, was starting to get crowded. The tribes nonetheless sought to continue the practice of capturing enemy horses, and their movements were anxiously noted in the frontier press. The Fort Benton, Montana, newspapers were in particularly close proximity to the action.

The Fort Benton *River Press* reported on June 14, 1882, in typical frontier fashion:

Another Indian Fight.

Clark Tingley [an early Montana pioneer] received a letter yesterday, written on the 30th, from a party at Fort Conrad (Kipp's post), stating that a short time prior to that date the Crees made another raid at the Blackfeet agency, getting away with a band of horses. They were followed by the Piegans [a Blackfeet subtribe] and overtaken near the Sweet Grass hills [near the Canadian border], where a battle took place, two of the Piegans being killed and one wounded. Whether or not the British reds [the Crees living north of the Canadian border] suffered any loss is not stated, nor are further details of the affair given. So long as they steal and kill one another, leaving the property of whites alone, the case is not so alarming. But the trouble is they don't always limit their devilish operations. Further trouble may now be expected.

A newsworthy account of a wide- ranging intertribal raid appeared on April 11, 1883:

THE RIVER PRESS.

Benton, Montana, Wednesday, April 11, 1883.

ANOTHER CREE RAID.

The British Devils Get Away with More American Horses.

Major Lincoln, Indian agent at Fort Belknap, received the following dispatch yesterday which fully explains itself:

FORT ASSINABOINE, April 4, '83.
Major Lincoln:

Mr. Fish reports per courier that a party of twelve Crees stole on the 1st inst. from the Gros Ventres, at People's creek, 67 head of horses, and proceeded northwest. I have sent courier to Fort Walsh at daylight with instructions to recover same. ILGES, Lieut. Col.

A forbearing people would like to know how long these raids by British subjects upon American soil are to continue with impunity. Wars have been raged for less infractions of international law, and yet the government takes not the least note of the oft repeated outrage!

The November 17, 1883, edition of the *Benton Weekly Record* carried this item:

We are informed by Cyprian Matt [an early Montana frontiersman] has started a town of his own at Warm Springs, at the head of the Little Rocky [Creek, in the Little Rocky Mountains in central Montana]. The settlement is composed of one cabin and twelve or fourteen lodges. A few nights ago some marauding Indians, supposed to be Crees, stole fourteen horses from Bird Chief, a Gros Ventre [Atsina, or "White Clay"] Indian, who was camped at Matt's place.

Another account, this time from the Fort Benton *River Press* on July 30, 1884, under the headline "Raiding Reds":

One day last week a party of Crows passed through the Judith Gap and had three fresh scalps—probably the locks of Piegan braves. At their camp on the Musselshell they had a scalp dance and a big time generally. It is about time that the settlers should put an end to these raids after the manner in which the cowboys are settling with the white horse thieves.

Stolen Horses, by Charles M. Russell (1911). Courtesy of C.M. Russell Museum, Great falls, MT.

On November 5, 1885, the newly-established Billings (Mont.) *Daily Gazette* reported via the Bozeman *Avant Courier*:

> We are reliably informed that on the 27th ult., near Sweet Grass, a fight took place between a band of Crow and Piegan Indians, in which one of the marauding Piegans was sent to the "happy hunting grounds" by the Winchester route. This decided the conflict in favor of the Crows, who followed up their victory by recovering 40 head of horses that the Piegans had stolen, and with which they were endeavoring to escape. The fight will probably be renewed at no distant date.

In 1884, a gold rush was on in the Little Rocky Mountains, at that time part of the vast northern Montana tribal hunting ground. White treasure seekers poured into the small, isolated mountain range illegally. By 1886, the colorful, and sometimes deadly, sport of native horse capture was fast coming to a close, for agitation was heard in Washington to reduce the huge tribal domain and open the Milk River country to white settlement.

The following year, the federal government divided the former common hunting grounds into the Blackfeet Reservation on the Rocky Mountain Front, the Fort Belknap Reserve for the Assinniboine and Gros Ventre (Atsina) Tribes on the Milk River and the Little Rocky Mountains in north-central Montana, and the Fort Peck Reservation isolating the Assiniboines and Sioux in northeastern Montana along the Missouri River. The tribes, in the recent past often at war with each other, were now secluded on their own reserves hundreds of miles apart.

From three remote forts, the U.S. Army patrolled the wide expanse between the reserves, making inter-tribal horse capture nearly impossible. The final intertribal raid was thought to have occurred in 1888 or 1889, when a Blood (a Blackfeet subtribe) or Sioux war party captured between 35 and 45 horses from the Crow reservation in southern Montana. The Crow warrior Two Leggings led four others in following the raiders, killing some, and recaptured many horses. An intercepting military unit recaptured ten horses, but the remaining members of the war party escaped to Canada, where three were arrested by authorities there.

The tribes, their proud spirits bowed but not broken, were confined behind the reservation fence, their age-old life now under the yoke of the federal government. Horses were still revered; their use was continued for ranch operations on tribal land. The affinity between the Native tribes and their horses continues to this day.

COUNTING COUP ON THE PIONEERS, or, TROUBLE ON THE "MEDICINE LINE"

In the early 17th Century, as the Spaniards were reintroducing horses to the "New World," restless Europeans began to explore and settle on the Atlantic seaboard. These new emigres came for other ostensible opportunities besides precious metals and conversion of souls. The English sailed for Massachusetts Bay Colony for religious freedom (within strict limits); Virginia was intended as a commercial venture. The French claimed the St. Lawrence River to expand trade in the North American interior. The Dutch, always in pursuit of business, settled in the Hudson River Valley.

After the first legendary Thanksgiving at Plymouth Rock, with the kindly Massasoit, a Wampanoag Native, supplying much of the provender, relations between the Native tribes and the European newcomers deteriorated rapidly. By 1637, the Natives in the Connecticut River valley and the New England settlers were actively at war. The year 1690 ushered in what may be called the first real world war, where, in New York, Pennsylvania, New England, and Quebec, the Iroquois Confederation played the English and French against each other for over seventy years.

The birth of the United States of America did not stanch the conflict; in fact, it was exacerbated. The ascendant American government subjugated the tribes south of the Mason-Dixon Line and westward from the Ohio River. One by one the tribes of the eastern and southern woodlands were forced from their homelands to present-day Oklahoma, at that time called "Indian Territory." The newly-vacated areas were opened to settlement and/or slavery.

The area west of the Missouri River was considered to be an utter wasteland, the "Great American Desert," a formidable barrier to be crossed in order to reach the Pacific Ocean. However, by 1840, Oregon was known to contain rich farmland, and more and more settlers were willing to cross the arid Great Plains to reach their "promised land." Intending to stay, they brought their furniture and livestock. In 1847, the Mormons, looking for a safe haven, reached the Salt Lake Valley—an area that would be soon be part of the Mexican Cession. The final piece was provided by the California gold rush beginning in 1848. The Great Plains tribes, like the Pueblos three centuries before, were in a vise, their domains under immediate threat from east and west. To the American people, stoked by the new secular religion called "Manifest Destiny," all that was necessary was to "fill in the blanks."

The Rocky Mountain Front was ideal hunting ground for the Native tribes. Many tribes from both sides of the mountains sought the American bison, the staff of life, keeping wary eyes out for the haughty Blackfeet. However, white traders, with their iron goods, trinkets, and whiskey, had had a transitory presence since the 1830s. The tribes traded buffalo robes and other pelts to the frontiersmen, becoming reliant on the new consumer goods. As a result, the wilderness economy was altered forever.

The Montana gold rush hastened the transition. In 1862, two brothers, James and Granville Stuart, prospected for gold along Grasshopper Gulch, near present-day Dillon, Montana, at that time part of Washington Territory. Finding paydirt, word soon spread, and within a few months the wild and remote camp of Bannock sprang up in the homeland of the Shoshoni subtribe of that name. Shortly thereafter, another bonanza was discovered in Alder Gulch about seventy-five miles away; the camp soon became known as Virginia City, now in the newly established Montana Territory. (Virginia City was originally named for Varina, Jefferson Davis' wife, by some Confederate sympathizers during the Civil War. The name was soon changed.)

For the newly established mining camps in the new Montana settlements, supplies and provisions were distant, scarce, and expensive. In short order, frontier entrepreneurs initiated new trade routes that would bring in supplies by freight wagon. (One of these routes, to Salt Lake City, was infested by "road agents" who would frequently rob the wagon trains. These were dealt with sternly by the "Vigilantes of Montana," and hanged from "fatal trees." At least that's the folklore.) Fresh meat was especially sought after, and was herded from Oregon, and, soon thereafter, from Texas. This was the start of the fabled Montana beef industry.

Freight was also brought to the camps, now proliferating, via steamboats plying the Missouri River from Saint Louis, Missouri. Soon Fort Benton, established in 1847 at the head of navigation on the Missouri River, became a thriving, colorful, and sometimes violent metropolis in the heart of "Indian Country." A wide-ranging trade empire radiated from Fort Benton: supplying the gold camps to the south, Idaho and Washington Territories to the west, the cosmopolitan cities in the East, and the illicit Canadian whiskey trade to the north via the infamous Whoop-Up Trail.

A Canadian account of Fort Benton, excerpted from the *Benton Weekly Record* from November 24, 1881, reads in part:

> Fort Benton is a frontier town about the size of Bismarck, with a population at present of about 1,500. Its population, like that of all frontier towns, is mixed in its origin. The occupations of the people are varied, and the antecedents of many of them it is better not to trace. Drinking shops and gambling houses form prominent features of the place. It is the head of navigation on the Missouri, and is the principal depot of the fur and wool trade; every steamer (of which during the short season of navigation some three of four leave weekly for Bismarck) carries several thousand skins and large quantities of wool. . . .

In 1868, a cavalry post, known as Fort Shaw, was established to protect freight roads from Fort Benton. It was centrally located in the Sun River Valley, about twenty-five miles from the Great Falls of the Missouri. From there, in January, 1870, Col. Baker's troops shamefully massacred 173 of Heavy Runner's band of friendly Piegan Natives in their winter camp near the Marias River. Shortly thereafter, President Grant opened the Sun and Teton River Valleys to white settlement.

The picturesque Sun River Valley (west of present-day Great Falls), although still in the heart of "Indian Country," was a stockgrowers' paradise—wide, fertile, and blessed with a fairly moderate climate. It also straddled several major trade routes, had plenty of room for expansion, and was under immediate military protection. Its nutritious prairie grasses had been worked by the American bison for millennia. Around 1870, a few settlers filtered into the Sun River valley, followed by more and more. By 1875, the Sun River Valley, along with the neighboring Teton, was supplying Helena and Fort Benton with all the beef they desired. Horses, a necessary adjunct to ranching operations, were also present in abundance, their immediate ancestors likely pulling freight wagons or employed by the Army.

In the mid-1870s, ranches were strung along the Sun, Teton, and Missouri River valleys, adjacent to the vast tribal hunting ground to the north. The tribal warriors were expected to stay in their homeland, and to leave the pioneers alone. The United States Army, soon with several additional outposts (Fort Keogh just west of present-day Miles City; Fort Custer at Hardin; Fort Assinaboine, near Havre; and Fort Maginnis east of Lewistown) was to keep peace on the frontier, to mediate disagreements between the various tribes, and also between the tribes and the pioneers. Most of these disputes involved the ownership of horses.

The newly arrived ranchmen owned vast herds of both horses and cattle, and often sheep. Isolated in lonely valleys and coulees, their nearest neighbors could be miles away. The Natives used age-old thoroughfares when crossing the prairies in search of buffalo and mischief. Once off the northern tribal domain, many of these routes ran through rangelands used to graze livestock. Conflict between the Native tribes and stockmen was inevitable.

The tribesmen still thought of horses as a source of wealth and prestige. The domesticated horses of the ranchers proved to be easy and irresistible targets for the Natives supposed to be confined to the north of the Marias and Missouri Rivers. The dynamic was changing from inter-tribal raids (which still happened frequently) to the easy pickings of the ranchers. The Natives still had a strong desire for captured horseflesh.

Another factor was in play: the "Medicine Line," the essentially open Canadian border a little more than a hundred miles to the north of Fort Benton. The tribes knew the border well, along with its significance: the United States Army could not cross the line. If Native tribesmen could cross the line with purloined horses then the Canadian authorities had jurisdiction, adding another dimension to the cat-and-mouse game.

The procedure for counting coup on the ranchmen was pretty much the same as against tribal rivals, having been perfected over the course of a century. A sleeping ranch could be considered a "sitting duck." Typical raids took place before dawn. Corrals were quietly opened or fences dismantled. The horses were herded out of the enclosure and into the open prairie, and off they went. Sometimes the Natives were caught in the act and gunfire exploded in the night. At other times, by the time the stockman realized what happened, his horses may have been twenty miles away, on their way over the border.

At this point, the rancher faced a dilemma. On one hand, he could follow the trail northward and hope to intercept the war party (a long shot) or head for the Blackfeet Agency, or to Forts Walsh or McLeod, Canadian police outposts in the Northwest Territory, now southern Alberta. Another option was to notify the American military authorities who would follow the raiders but were required to halt at the "Medicine Line." Most often the ranchers would choose the former.

After a chase that could cover hundreds of miles, the pursuers sometimes located their horses. The U.S. tribal agent or Canadian mounted policemen would accompany the aggrieved rancher as he searched for his brand among what could be hundreds of confiscated horses. He rode back to his ranch, generally several days away, angry with the Natives and generally disgusted with the state of affairs.

The Fort Benton newspapers carried frequent and colorful accounts of the losses of the pioneer ranchers. Written in the vernacular of the day, these news articles provide a thorough written record of the perils of being a stockman on the "Lonesome Prairie."

From the establishment of the newspapers, the accounts were nearly constant. Vol. I, No. 1 of the *Benton Record* noted five horses stolen by Gros Ventres Natives. From that point, the Montana press ran such items for over a decade.

The Benton Record.

VOL. III FORT BENTON, M. T., FRIDAY, AUGUST 24 1877. NO. 13.

From the Record Extra.]

THE STORM BREWING.

Indications of an Out-
break Among the
Gros Ventres, As-
sinaboins and
Piegus.

SITTING BULL AT FORT PECK.

Nez Perce Scouts on
the Marias River

Sixty Horses Stol-
en from the 28-
Mile Springs
& Blackfoot
Agency.

FIRING THE PRAIRIE.

Alarm at Sun River.

THE BLACKFOOT TREATY.

Weekly headline describing the agitated state of affairs in Northern Montana.

A typical account of horses lost to raiding Natives appeared in the May 17, 1882, issue of the *River Press*:

Raided by Redskins.

On Thursday night of last week the Indians raided a number of ranches on the Teton and succeeded in getting away with quite a band of horses. Mr. J.D. Weatherwax is short six head of work horses, taken out of his corral; John Galbreath loses 22 head and a fine stallion, which was taken from his stall; Niquette finds four of his animals are gone, and others in that locality we believe, are losers. The raid was made with such skill and adroitness that the loss was not discovered until the next morning, when the rascally reds were many miles away. The raiding party are known to be Crees, belonging on the other side of the line, where, it seems, they manage to get rid of all the animals they can steal on this side. Within the last year Mr. Weatherwax's ranch has been raided three times and his horses stolen, and naturally enough, he begins to think that the business is getting a little monotonous. In would not be difficult to induce him to take the war path.

Another report from the December 13, 1882 edition of the *River Press* reads:

THE RIVER PRESS.

Benton, Montana, Wednesday, December 13, 1882.　　No. 3.

Horse Stealing by Indians.

Henry Niehoff who returned with his train from Fort Belknap yesterday, informed a RIVER PRESS reporter that on Friday last a band of Cree Indians stole all of the horses belonging to a party of twelve lodges of Gros Ventres who were camped on Big Birch creek, setting them a foot entirely. The Crees were superior in number and boldly rode up to the camp in broad day light and made off with the animals. But not satisfied with this conquest they stole "every hoof" at the sheep ranch on Beaver creek—owned by a number of officers at Fort Assinaboine—and doubtless long before this are on the queen's soil, their native heath, enjoying the success of their southern excursion. Some seven or eight horses were taken from the sheep ranch, and the prospects of their recovery are not very flattering.

Robert Jackson who came in from the Marias yesterday, states that several days ago a party of Piegans stole twenty-five head of horses at his place. He followed them to the agency and recovered nine head, all he could find there. Proceeding thence to "Black Weasel's" camp on the Marias he found the rest of his horses, as well as others that had been stolen from white men, but the rascally reds refused to deliver them up, with exception of the chief who turned over the animal that had been given him.

Horse stealing by Indians is becoming altogether too frequent in northern Montana, and something should be done to punish the thieves and thus put a check on this bad business.

This item, from the June 14, 1882, edition of the *River Press* relates a more fortunate outcome than most:

More Horses recovered from the Crees.

On the 11th of May ten head of horses were stolen by Indians from Messrs Simmons and Martin, of the Marias. The former followed in pursuit, and we are glad to state has recovered his horses with the exception of two head. As in the case of the Teton ranchmen who had horses stolen, Col. Irvine did all in his power to recover the stolen property and in each case was successful. He proposes, so far as lies in his power, to give the citizens of Montana no cause for complaint on this score, and his commendable action whenever called upon is certainly an evidence of the fact. Whoever loses horses through the agency of the thieving Crees can count on Col. Irvine as a valuable assistant in recovering the same. In behalf of the stockmen of Montana we return him a vote of thanks.

The tribal hunting ground of northern Montana was (and is) a vast treeless prairie, a nearly limitless grassland teeming with wildlife, a (generally) full larder for survival. It was relatively flat in some areas but quite rugged in others, interrupted by dry drainages and alkaline streams. The horizon is punctuated by scattered mountain ranges: the Bear Paws, Little Rockies, and Sweet Grass Hills near the "Medicine Line," ideal refuges for tribal vision quests and ceremonies. It has a stark, isolated beauty, the feel of infinity.

The Milk River was the main stream through the huge reservation. Flowing for over three hundred miles, it was mostly slow, sluggish, and narrow. It had a color of what Meriwether Lewis described as a cup of tea with milk, a stark contrast to the clear mountain streams along the Rocky Mountain Front. During floods, most every spring, it grew to a muddy, frothy torrent, miles across, but its meandering valley was considered prime buffalo hunting ground.

In frontier times the area was completely devoid of settlement, and for that matter, pioneer interest. The extreme climate, 110° in the summer to -60° in the winter, hampered active exploration. In the arid climate, water was often many miles away, but in rainy weather, which is seldom, the clay soil become impassible for days or weeks. The rugged terrain precluded all but the most labor-intensive (and dangerous) transportation. The area was left to the tribes.

Its isolation was conducive to any number of schemes, mostly involving smuggling, stolen horses, and illicit whiskey. The U.S. military had a hard time patrolling the reserve, especially the eastern portion, often hundreds of rugged miles from their bases. It was virtually impossible to monitor illegal activity, which as time went on became more prevalent.

In about 1877, a trading post sprang up in the Big Bend of the Milk River at the site of an old tribal ceremonial ground. Located northeast of present-day Malta, its exact origin as a storehouse lost to antiquity, it became known as "Medicine Lodge." One of the few vestiges of "civilization" in the heart of buffalo country, its humble beginnings consisted of a main trading post associated with small groups of cabins along the Milk River for a few miles. Its denizens were Crees and Metís (French *voyageurs* married to Cree women) for the most part, but the adjacent hunting grounds drew members of other tribes and traders over a wide area from both sides of the border. Its currency was buffalo robes, but whiskey and stolen horses were important drawing cards. Over time, Medicine Lodge grew to a fairly substantial settlement, without law or civil authority.

Medicine Lodge was a volatile mix in the middle of nowhere. Within a short time it became a depôt for stolen horses as a way station over the "Medicine Line," less than forty miles away by way of Frenchman and Woody Island Creeks. It was a gathering point for many tribes who didn't necessarily get along. In addition to the local tribes, the Crees, Gros Ventres, and Assinniboines, the Big Bend country was frequented by hostile Natives from the south who were on the lam after the "Sioux Wars."

Being over 200 miles from any newspaper, little is known about day-to-day life in Medicine Lodge. It seems fair to say that its main source of income was the buffalo that were still abundant in the area at that late date. Smaller game was also plentiful. The thick cottonwoods along the river were cut down for cabins and firewood during the frigid winters. From time to time, freight wagons arrived from Fort Belknap carrying supplies and departed loaded with buffalo robes. Barrels of whiskey, brought from landings and wood yards on the Missouri River, were undoubtedly eagerly awaited. Tribal relatives from both sides of the line came and went. It can be assumed that drinking, gambling, and horse racing were principal pastimes, along with the attendant shootings and "cutting affrays."

In March of 1882, J.J. Healy, a noted frontiersman and sheriff of Choteau (at that time the correct spelling) County, along with two deputies, left Fort Benton for Medicine Lodge to investigate possible smuggling activity and to collect taxes (!). Not even certain that he had jurisdiction in what he thought might be the adjacent Dawson County (it was), Healy went about his duties anyway, confiscating buffalo robes in lieu of cash. The disgusted Natives captured Healy and his deputies and locked them in a cabin. Several days into his captivity, Healy was able to bribe one of his captors (with buffalo robes, of course) to ride ninety miles to Wolf Point, and to notify the authorities of his predicament. In due time, an army captain arrived in Medicine Lodge and liberated Healy and his deputies. Shortly thereafter the U.S. Army from Fort Assinaboine (at that time the correct spelling) raided Medicine Lodge and scattered its residents to the wind.

But not for long. The *Benton Record*, in its edition of May 4, 1882, reported:

BACK AGAIN.

Medicine Lodge Again Infested With Half-Breeds—Big Bear on Beaver Creek Defies the Authorities—Holding up Prairie Travelers.

. . . Murray Nicholson and Pete Shambo on a scout for the government, accompanied the wagon [to return stores to Fort Belknap] for part of the way to Medicine Lodge. They report that Big Bear [a Cree Chief] is again back in his old position on Beaver Creek about half way down the Big Bend of Milk river; that there are plenty of buffalo there, and he declared he has no intention of going across the line. Medicine Lodge is again overrun with half-breeds [Metís], and Soto and Cree Indians, the same outfit which the Assinnaboine expedition drove across the line a short time ago. They have all come back again and will camp there all summer, they say.

In the summer of 1882, military authorities at Fort Assinaboine sent two cavalry troops and four infantry companies to set up camp in the Big Bend of the Milk River. From this point the U.S. Army was able to stanch the illegal activity at Medicine Lodge and to make sure the Cree and Metís Natives, as British subjects, stayed on their side of the line. On October 4, 1882, the *River Press* contained an article entitled: **NO MORE A THIEVES' RETREAT. The Camp on Milk River Accomplished Much Good, and Will Soon be Abandoned.**

THE RIVER PRESS.

Benton, Montana, Wednesday, October 4, 1882.   No. 50.

NO MORE A THIEVES' RETREAT.

The Camp on Milk River Has Accomplished Much Good, and Will Soon Be Abandoned.

Late dispatches from the summer camp at the Big Bend of the Milk river, says the *Pioneer Press*, have been received, which indicate a satisfactory condition of affairs in that section, heretofore the haunt of half-breed smugglers and Indian raiders and horse thieves. The camp was established early in July last by troops from Fort Assinaboine, consisting of troops L and H, Second cavalry, and companies A, F, H and K, Eighteenth infantry, under the command of Capt. E. R. Kellogg, Second cavalry, for the purpose of holding in check the Indians from the British possessions and keeping them from hunting and committing depredations on this side of the boundary line. The purpose of the movement has been pretty effectually accomplished and the Indians have given the camp a wide berth. There has been considerable scouting during the last two months, but apart from this the only thing resembling active warfare took place soon after their arrival at Big Bend, when Capt. Kellogg pursued and captured a party of twenty-four Crees and six half-breeds, disarmed them and sent them over the border. Scouts have recently come into Big Bend with the news that Big Bear, who essays the role of Sitting Bull in that region with the band of Little Pine Crees, has left his camp near the boundary and gone to Fort Walsh. In view of this change of base, and the near approach of cold weather, it is understood that the camp at Big Bend will be abandoned about the 1st of October, and a portion of Capt. Kellogg's command will be stationed at some point within easy communication with and nearer Fort Assinaboine. The remainder will return to the fort.

Two weeks later, on October 18, the River Press reported:

All Quiet on Milk River.

Telegraphic advices have been received at department headquarters at Fort Snelling [in Minnesota] from Col. Thomas H. Ruger, Eighteenth infantry, commanding the district of Montana, which report a peaceful and satisfactory state of affairs throughout the district, and on this account, and because the season for active operations is nearly over, it has been decided to call in the various detachments now in the field and place them in winter quarters. . . .

Within a short time, buffalo would become scarce in the vast grasslands along the border, and a gathering place would be unnecessary in the Big Bend. The last buffalo was slaughtered along the Milk River in 1885. Medicine Lodge faded into history.

The winter of 1883 saw one of the greatest tragedies in American history. The buffalo had virtually vanished from the northern Great Plains, only a few scattered bands widely dispersed. For some reason (no doubt there was plenty of blame to go around), the United States government failed to provide enough annuities at the Blackfeet Agency. By January of 1884, the Natives were quickly running out of beef and flour. By the end of winter hundreds of them were starving. Not only were they physically defeated, but their proud spirit was essentially broken by the "Starvation Winter." From that time forward, they remained close to their agency near the Rocky Mountain Front. Within a short time, the legendary Blackfeet horse-capturing raids almost totally came to an end.

North of the border, the Crees and Metís were facing their own challenges. Chafing under British rule, they were determined to ensure their basic human rights. Louis Riel, born in Quebec and ordained as a Catholic priest, was regarded by the Natives as somewhat of a mystic. Riel, with a charismatic persona, became a spiritual leader to the High Plains tribes in Canada. A veteran of the agitation which created the Province of Manitoba in 1870, he continued to press for tribal rights.

In the spring of 1885, the Crees, under their chiefs Big Bear and Poundmaker, engaged Canadian soldiers in a series of short but bloody skirmishes. At Batouche, in present-day southern Alberta, a battle took place where the tribesmen got the upper hand early, only to run out of ammunition. After their victory by default, the Canadian government came down hard on the Native Americans, who were confined to barren and desolate reserves on the cold northern Great Plains. Utterly defeated, many Crees and Metís migrated over the border where they were icily received by the American pioneers. They set up camps along the Milk River and drifted from town to town in northern Montana. In 1896, the U.S. Army loaded them into railroad cars and escorted them back to Canada, and being unwelcome there, they quickly returned, landless and shunned wherever they went. Finally, in 1916, the federal government (over the objections of the newly arrived homesteaders) created the Rocky Boys Indian Reservation for the Crees and the Ojibwa (Chippewa) tribe, some of them relocated from the overcrowded Turtle Mountain reserve in North Dakota.

This combination of events finally extinguished the tribal raids on pioneer horses, although scattered raids continued until about 1892. After the Milk River country was opened to ranching in 1888, the tribes, confined to their own reservations, were faced to scratch for their very survival. The pioneers breathed a sigh of relief, their property safe from tribal depredations.

THE QUEST FOR PROFIT, or, TURNING HORSETHIEVES INTO ANGELS

5

brief sidebar:

It's safe to say that the Industrial Revolution began in the War Between the States. Railroads, first chartered in the U.S. in 1827, were steadily connecting the cities of the East (the South was a somewhat different scenario). Large businesses, such as Brooks Brothers (for military uniforms) and DuPont (for explosives) can be considered among the first megacorporations.

After the Confederate surrender, other industries followed their example. Railroad building became a national obsession. The steel industry initially focused on creating iron rails, finding ready constumers among the railroads. Huge manufacturing facilities sprang up to build locomotives and rolling stock. Civil engineers designed bridges and tunnels.

Cyrus McCormick patented the mechanical reaper in 1834; in the 1837, John Deere invented the self-scouring plow, which, while not exactly making farming easier, made it more efficient. Later, in 1874, J.F. Glidden obtained the first patent for barbed wire, the "wire that won the West," that did more than its share to pit stockgrowers and farmers against one another.

In 1866, Nelson Story brought a herd of about 1,000 cattle from Texas to the Gallatin Valley in Montana, and within a short time, ranching became an industry rather than a pursuit, financed in large part by Eastern and foreign capital.

By the early 1880s, the western frontier was beginning, just beginning, to lose its edge. In the north, the plains tribes were subdued and assigned to reservations on lands thought to be useless for profit; in the Southwest, the Native tribes were in the final throes of their resistance. The buffalo had been exterminated—almost the entire species. The landscape was nearly vacant, but it would not remain that way for long.

Eastern industrialists, fueled by a fevered display of "Social Darwinism," rushed to fill the vacuum. Instead of a tractless void, it was discovered that the American West was filled with a trove of what was thought to be inexhaustible resources.

One of these was grass, growing high as a man on spongy soil that had never been disturbed. To supply a national insatiability for beef, cattle herds were trailed northward from Texas for "finishing" on the lush grasslands of Montana and Wyoming, and subsequently shipped by rail to the Dickinsonian packing districts in the Midwest.

Horses were necessary for ranching operations. Cattle were well adapted to the vast open grassland, now free of buffalo, but require constant attention. Horses, being easily herded, seemingly had an instinct for herding livestock in turn. When properly trained a good cow horse could cut a single animal out of a herd of thousands, if needed. A cowboy and his horse became vital companions while tending herds, and his sure-footed horse could be relied upon when heading off a stampede caused by lightning in the middle of the night. Horses were necessary to gather cattle over vast areas, whether to the branding fire in the spring or off to market in the fall. On the open range, a horse and rider needed to have a mutual respect and reliance on one another. Either had to be counted on to save the other's life if need be, and they both knew it.

By 1884, ranching had grown into a widespread industry in Central and Eastern Montana (north of the Missouri and Marias Rivers was still the vast tribal hunting ground). Well-financed operations were headquartered at springs or water-courses, and livestock were grazed on free government land. Cattle were left to their own devices as they were fattened for market; accounting was based on the spring and fall roundups. Some losses were to be expected from natural causes.

As the ranching industry gained a foothold on the Northern plains, another European characteristic soon emerged: the mercantile instinct. Horses were known for their usefulness, and as such, their monetary value. Buying and selling horses became commonplace, and horse thievery grew apace. By the early 1880s, the stolen horse trade became a real issue. Dishonest cowboys, in a somewhat vagabond occupation, would drift across the prairie, seizing untended horses when the opportunity arose. These ne'er-do-wells, often outlaws in their own right, became unwelcome in their vast new home.

These outlaws rode in from far and wide. Although they resided on the margins of society, their backgrounds can occasionally be traced. The soon-to-be mentioned "Rattlesnake Jake" Owens grew up in Shreveport, Louisiana, and his compatriot, Charlie Fallon, had supposedly drifted north from Laredo, Texas; they were wanted in Wyoming Territory for horse theft. (At this point it is important to mention that in various accounts "Rattlesnake Jake" refers to Fallon. All sorts of misidentification appears in historical accounts.) Jack Stringer was thought to be well-educated but had a insatiable gambling habit. "Flopping Bill" Cantrell, from Tennessee, played both sides of the law. Undoubtedly, some of these men were Civil War veterans or deserters from both sides. There are many others, such as "California Ed," "Red Mike," "Swift Bill," and "Paddy Rose," whose nicknames are remembered but whose origins have been lost to antiquity.

Once they darkened the dootstep of Montana, they generally followed the pursuits of buffalo hunting, wolf trapping, cutting wood for steamboats, whiskey-running, gambling, and horse thievery. Established pioneers regarded them as low-lifes and menacing outcasts.

The tools for the vocation of horse thievery were simple: a rope, a swift and sure-footed horse, basic cowboying skills such as roping and cutting, a "running iron" (generally a single bar brand, used to alter identifying marks on animals) or a frying pan (to rebrand circles), the ability to work under the cover of darkness, a network of questionable co-conspirators, and a safe place to hide. Stealing horses was a perilous career. While the rewards could be considerable, the work was fraught with occupational hazards.

As time went on, the trade became more organized. Stolen horses were secreted in isolated areas like those of the Missouri Breaks (the wild labyrinth along the Missouri River in Montana), generally located near steamboat wood yards often operated by men of questionable character. There the brands were altered to give the horses' ownership a supposed legitimacy. (The thieves' customers were not generally too picky about this.) From there, the horses were driven across Indian Country to Canada, or more perilously, into Wyoming or Dakota. As part of a far-flung network, horses stolen in Canada, Wyoming, or Dakota were moved via the reverse route.

An informative article appeared in the September 27, 1882, edition of the Fort Benton *River Press:*

"BIG JEFF."

The Leader of a Band of Horse Thieves and How He Conducts His Operations.

… Jeff with a band of possibly a dozen congenial companions are located at the general crossing of the Musselshell where they have rather rude and temporary accommodations for themselves but a large and very fine corral for their horses. Their business, pure and simple, as we are informed, is to steal horses and dispose of them. The Judith Basin[,] Musselshell, Yellowstone, and Missouri valleys are their fields of operations, and the numerous reports of horse stealing in these valleys go to indicate a large and prosperous business. When they steal an animal north of their rendezvous they send him south for sale or sell him to some wayfarer going in that direction or *vice versa*, thus avoiding to a great extent any trouble from parties in search for their animals. If officers appear in that section the band scatters out in various directions and they have no difficulty in keeping out of the way—but it is rarely that they are troubled. They are desperate men, and it would require no ordinary posse to capture them. …

The early Territorial court system was woefully inadequate in the face of the burgeoning horse thievery trade. The counties were too sparsely populated and distances too great—the mouth of the Musselshell was at least a hundred and forty miles from any county seat—for the court to have any real effectiveness. Horse-stealing prosecutions were few and far between, with convictions resulting in short sentences—generally a year in the penitentiary. Horse thieves knew this, and liked the odds.

In the winter of 1884 the Montana Stockgrowers' Association was organized, featuring such historical luminaries as Granville Stuart, Pierre Wibaux, Theodore Roosevelt, and the Marquis de Mores from Dakota Territory. Its main purpose was to foster political influence in the Territorial Legislature and, acknowledging the inadequacy of the territorial court system, to confront the pesky and growing problem of range theft.

Trouble was not long in coming. On February 14, 1884, in the small hamlet of Stoneville (now Alzada), Montana, a group of horse thieves, led by George Axelby, sought to "rescue" Jesse Purdon, one of their fraternity, from a Miles City sheriff's posse taking him toward Deadwood, Dakota Territory, to face charges of horse stealing on the reservation. At Stoneville, a convenient midpoint, the posse was met by another to take Purdon the rest of the way to Deadwood. In a gun battle near the saloon in the small town, a Dakota deputy named Jack O'Hara was shot dead by "Billy the Kid," an Axelby cohort. A cowboy employed by the nearby Driskill "D" Ranch, up the Little Missouri River, was shot down in front of the saloon. That night, Jack Campbell, another member of the gang, was killed in a running gun battle down the Little Missouri, and Harry Tuttle was badly wounded. Tuttle was taken to a Deadwood hospital, where on February 27 he was removed by masked men wearing buffalo robes and hanged from a nearby tree. Axleby, thought to be wounded in the running battle, was supposed to have ridden to his hideout near Devil's Tower, where he vanished from history.

Things simmered for a while, until June of 1884 when the *Bismarck Weekly Tribune*, in its June 27th edition, reported that:

> . . . The body of O'Neil, who was hung to a telegraph pole between Miller and Victoria, was buried Monday, the verdict of the jury that he came to his death by hanging. [!] When found his hands were tied behind him and his feet were tied together. A belt was about his waist filled with loaded shells, and a placard was on his clothes bore the words, "Jack O'Neil the horse thief." A number of people have recognized him as O'Neil the horse thief, and say that he has been a bad character for years. . . .

Shortly thereafter the July 2nd issue of the *River Press* carried an account of eight horses stolen from the Billings and Benton Stage Company at Lavina. A posse of about fifteen found:

> ". . . two riders driving a small band of horses. The thieves, upon becoming aware that they were observed by the cowboys, evidently thinking that they were in pursuit, quickly dismounted and commenced changing their saddles and other equipments to fresh horses. This caused the cowboys to suspect they were horse thieves, and they immediately gave chase. . . . One mile from where the first encounter took place they again overhauled the fleeing desperadoes.
>
> The particulars of the killing we have been unable to learn, but the boys returned with the eight horses, and the two horses rode by the thieves, also their guns and revolvers— in fact, their full accoutrements. They will not say that they killed their men, but there is no doubt of the fact. They do say, however, that Owens and Nickerson will steal no more horses. . . ."

The same edition contained another report from a different quarter:

THE HANGMAN'S NOOSE.

Two Suffer the Penalty of Death at Judith Landing for Horse Stealing.

JUDITH LANDING, June 30, 1884.

Editors of the River Press:

Narcisse Laverdure, a half-breed, was hung here at 2 o'clock a.m. on the 27th inst. For horse stealing, and his uncle, Leo Laverdure, was shot and instantly killed while attempting to escape on the morning of the 28th. The particulars are as follows: On the morning of the 28th inst. The half-breeds ran off five head of horses from the opposite side of the river, belonging to J.A. Wells [a well-known frontiersman]. When out about eleven miles they accidentally came across William Thompson, who, knowing the horses, ordered them to halt. This they refused to do and attempted to escape. Thompson being well armed and on a good horse gave chase. They separated, and after a chase of six miles Thompson ran down Narcisse, Leo getting away. Thompson brought the prisoner and all the horses to this place. They were brought over the river in a skiff, Narcisse being well guarded in a stable. At 2 o'clock next morning the guards were overpowered by an armed posse of thirty men, and Laverdure was taken out and hung to an overspreading branch of a large cottonwood tree, and a card marked "Horse Thief" pinned to his back. Three men then started in pursuit of Leo, who was overtaken on Eagle Creek, and in trying to and in trying to escape was shot and instantly killed. . . .

On July 4th another assumed horse thief was found hanging to a tree near Fort Maginnis.

Up to that time, the extra-legal action was unorganized and far-flung. That was about to change.

On July 4, 1884, the nascent settlement of Lewistown, Montana, was holding a 4th of July event when two known toughs and suspected horse thieves, "Rattlesnake Jake" Owens and Charlie Fallon, were looking for trouble. In the subsequent melee, in the Maiden *Mineral Argus* on July 10 reported under the headline:

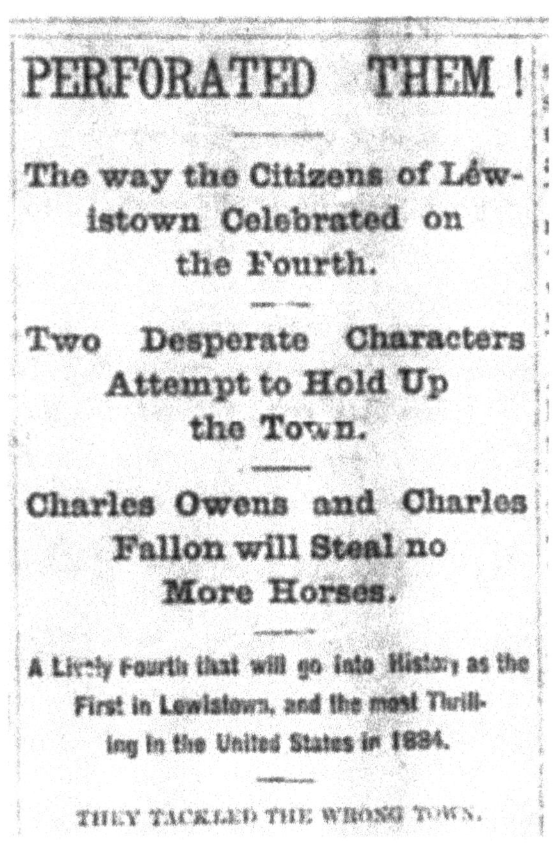

. . . A few minutes later they drove up town and entered Crowley & Kemp's saloon where they took three drinks apiece, remarkingwhile there that he would be perfectly satisfied if he could only kill that s-----of a b----half-breed, meaning John Doane (who had said nothing to him.) When Jake steped [sic] out of the saloon, Doane was standing at the door of T.C. Power& Bros. store. Jake steped up to him and whipping out his gun began firing, while Doane, at the same time threw up a small 32 caliber revolver and fired, hitting Jake in the forefinger of the left hand (the hand he held his gun in). He then took his revolver in his right hand and fired into the store at Doane. By this time the scramble for guns was general and shooting began in earnest. Fallon was on his horse in the act at discharging his Winchester at any one within range, when he was shot through the abdomen, causing him to fall forward on the horn of his saddle, and wheeling his horse started on a run up the street from the creek a distance of about 400 yards when he turned and returned to the rear of Ed. Clark's photograph tent, as shown by 01 in the diagram [shown below], where his pal (Designated by 0) had retreated to Power's store, and kneeling shooting at anyone in sight. Fallon dismounted, dropped on his knees, and taking deliberate aim with his rifle at a young man named Ben. Smith, who, with several others, was running to get out of the bullets that were whizzing in all directions, fired the ball striking Smith in the left cheek, coursing upward and lodged in the brain, caused instant death.

By this time citizens from behind saloons, barns, and Crowley & Kemps ice house were pouring a destructive fire into the doomed pair, who as long as they were able to pull a trigger, kept returning shot for shot.

Owens was the first to fall while Fallon bit the dust a few seconds later when the firing ceased and the bodies were taken care of—the desperadoes being removed to Power's old store room while the body of the unfortunate Smith was cared for by the Jackson Bros., in whose employ he was. . . .

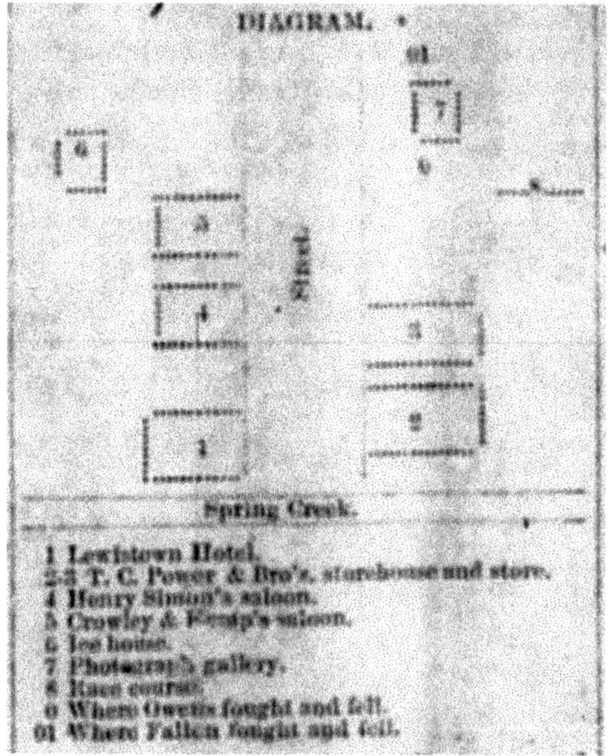

Diagram of the area.

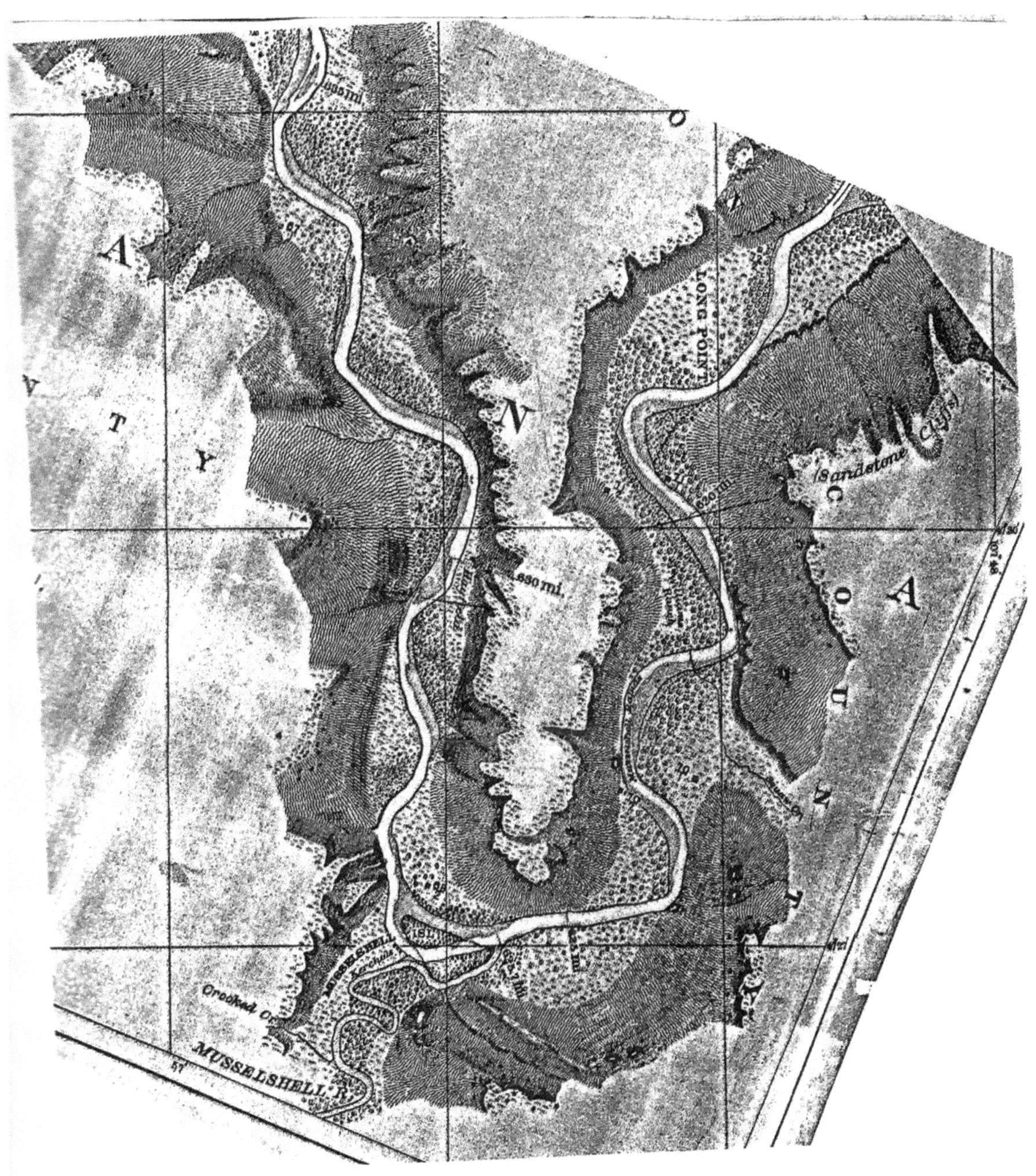

The Mouth of the Musselshell River, Montana. (Now known as UL Bend.)
1893 Missouri River Commission Map- Sheet 69.

The citizens were outraged. By and large, the settlers of eastern Montana were peaceable and law-abiding—they just wanted safe and stable surroundings where they could raise their families and earn a living. They felt like they were under siege from horse-thieves and outlaws, and they resented the idea of being prey to anyone.

Granville Stuart, a legendary Montana pioneer, was one of the organizers of the Montana Stockgrowers' Association. While he was never confirmed as a participant in the events of the tense summer of 1884, he was certainly a witness. They are recorded in his sprawling memoir, *Forty Years of the Frontier*, and largely parallel the accounts published in the newspapers.

Shortly after the gun battle in the dusty streets in Lewistown a group of cowboys in the hire of a few prominent ranchers of central Montana began meeting secretly with their employers. On July of 1884, this shadowy organization, with a wink and a nod from the Stockgrowers' Association, went to work in the Missouri Breaks. The group became informally known as "Stuart's Stranglers."

On the Fourth of July, a group of vigilantes arrived at the hideaway of Billy Downs at the mouth of the Musselshell River. At the same time, another party was dispatched toward Rocky Point, a rude wolfer's settlement on the river in the Missouri Breaks, cleaning out horse thieves and recovering stolen horses. After their work was done at those points, the parties made their way downstream fifteen miles to the abandoned woodyard at Bates Point at the mouth of Fourchette Creek, arriving on July 8. There they burned the cabin, stable, and firewood of one "Old Man James," his two sons, Jack Stringer, and several others. After the ensuing gun battle and extralegal hanging(s), the place was deserted. Some of the Bates Point outlaws escaped down the river, followed by the posse by raft toward Poplar Creek, considerably farther downstream.

The first action was reported in the *Mineral Argus* on July 17, 1884:

> Reese Anderson, of the firm of Stuart, Kohrs & Co., accompanied by several other well known cow-boys, pursued and overtook number of horse-thieves, who were driving a large band of horses into the Canadian Possessions, at the Little Rockey [*sic*] mountains, regaining 28 head of stock. Two of the thieves escaped mounted, while five or six succeeded in finding secure hiding places. 'Tis well that Reece and his brave associated did not find their retreat, a there would have been a few of "some ones' darlings" compelled to stretch hemp.

Soon other reports began filtering in to the newspapers. On July 23, 1884, the *River Press,* under the headline "The Hanging Down the River" came the following account:

> From Capt. Todd and other offices and passengers on the Batchelor [a Missouri River steamboat] we gleaned all that could be learned in reference to the reported lynching of five men down the river—it the vicinity of Rocky Point, as it was first reported here. No definite information on the subject could be secured by those on the boat, but rumors of all kinds were thick enough. Billy Downes and Charles Owens [?] are certainly among the victims. Sixteen men came to the former's place below the Musselshell, in the afternoon, and finding a number of horses they knew, picked them out and took them off some distance, returning soon afterward. They remained until evening, when they "invited" Downes and Owens to accompany them, which they did, of course. The men never returned and the plain inference is that they were lynched. Other places along the river were deserted, and there has been either a general

skipping out or cleaning out, which is not known at this writing. There was unusual reticence manifested at the different landings, and nothing of a definite nature has been learned. . . .

Another Rocky Point report appeared in the *Helena Weekly Herald* on July 24, 1884, carried some additional information:

HORSE THIEVES.

Five More Strung up at Rocky Point—Thirteen Lynched and Shot in Three Weeks.

[River Press.]

Dave Hilger and S. X. Swendeman, who arrived from Judith City yesterday, bring the startling information that five horse thieves were captured and hung in the vicinity of Rocky point a few days ago. The word was brought to Judith just as they were taking their departure, and they did not get the particulars of the extraordinary event. The deed was done by a regularly organized band of cow boys, who are out to round-up the thieves that infest that section, and they are doing their work in good shape. They secured thirty-two head of horses from the quintet of outlaws, and then made short work of them by hanging the lot to the nearest tree. While the details are not at hand, there seems to be no doubt whatever that the bill as given in general is a true one.

The stock men and other citizens are making it decidedly interesting for the outlaws that infest the region between the lower Judith and Musselshell. Within the past three weeks thirteen of them have been lynched, and it is probable the end is not yet. The campaign was opened by the killing of two thieves on the Musselshell; followed by the dispatch of two half-breeds at Clagett; then one was strung up on Armell creek and another near Fort Maginnis; two more were "fixed" at Lewiston on the Fourth, and the big haul at Rocky Point is the latest—making in all thirteen victims. At this rate it will not take long to clean out the gang, and it is the only effective way to do it.

An unsubstantiated rumor, from the *Glendive Independent,* appeared in the *River Press:*

More Angel Horse Thieves.

A band of horse thieves was followed from Bart Stow's wood yard, on Milk river, several days ago. The horses were recovered. The thieves were overtaken at Willow bu[n]ch, across the line, and two of them are said to be angels now.

On July 30, 1884, the *River Press* contained the following news:

The Raid on the Missouri River Horse Thieves.

. . . No definite information has been received as to operations down the river. The vigilantes, numbering fifteen or twenty fearless men, hailed the steamer Benton at old Fort Hawley last Tuesday to secure some provisions. They did not have much to say other that they were rounding up the horse thieves and still had some work before them. On Sunday, the 20th, they had a fight with the thieves at Bateman's wood yard that lasted two hours. It seems that a number of the thieves, probably twenty, had gathered here to make a stand against the vigilantes. They occupied a cabin and a tent some distance from the house. As a matter of safety they put out two sentries to look out for the cowboys, but the latter came up and took a position near the house without being seen, and at daylight opened fire on the thieves, protected by trees and stumps. The men in the tent were all killed and some of those in the cabin, the others escaping. The house and stable were burned. The names of the victims are not known, and in fact the details are of a meagre and indefinite order. . . The James place was totally destroyed by fire, including the wood, and it is believed that the father and two sons were killed. Two or three other wood yards were burned out. The "avengers" had a name and history of every one of the "gang" along the river, and they expressed a purpose of not letting up as long as there was one of them left. They expected to apply to the boat on its return trip for supplies "to carry on the war," and when they finish their work horse thieves will be as scarce on the upper Missouri river as they are in Heaven.

And this from the July 31, 1884, Maiden *Mineral Argus:*

. . . It seems that the pursuing party "gathered at the river" near the mouth of the Musselshell, where the Big Muddy "washes up its silver spray" and where one old man James has a ranch, and found a corral containing thirty or forty horses, some of which were recognized by the pursuers as their own. It being early in the morning that cabin and corral was surrounded and the first movement of the thieves anxiously awaited.

Old man James was first to emerge from the robber's lair, when the boys made him throw open the corral and turn the horses out. The rest of the thieves were asleep but the old man gave the alarm and two of his sons and four other men came to his assistance, but were driven back into the cabin instanter [sic], where they refused to surrender under any condition. All other efforts to bring them out proving futile, fire was set to the hay and corral, which being close to the cabin ignited that also, and the occupants seeing it was a "forced play" came out and surrendered or were shot at the threshold of the cabin—just how they were dispatched we are unable to state, but as they were seen hanging to trees, a brief examination was doubtless given and the tree decorating begun. . . .

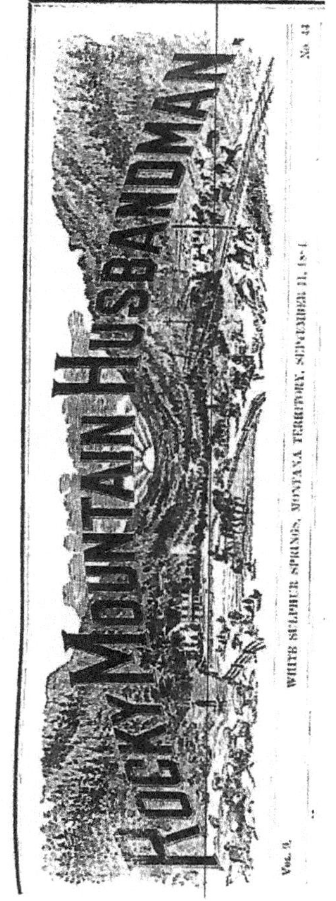

STOLEN HORSES.

The following is a list of horses captured from horse thieves and to be found at Stuart, Kohrs & Co's, ranch, near Fort Maginnis:

One dun horse, about 16 hands high, four white feet, dark mane and tail, no brands. One light brown horse, freshly branded HB combined on left shoulder, and 217 B on left fore hoof; about 16 hands high. One sorrel horse, about 15 hands high, branded HP combined (fresh) on left shoulder; both hind feet and left fore foot white; apparently 217 B has been erased from left fore foot. One dark bay horse, about 16 hands high, right hind foot white; freshly branded HB combined on left shou'der and 217 on left fore hoof. One flea-bitten gray horse, about 16 hands high; freshly branded HP combined over a dash on left shoulder over dim MP brand; also 217 on left hoof. One bay horse, about 16 hands high, blind in right eye, branded dim 2 B on left thigh. One bright bay horse, about 15 hands high, branded TH combined on left thigh and ≣‖≣ on left shoulder; also 2 on left side of neck. One dun horse, stripe in face, branded C on left shoulder, and 45 connected and S on right shoulder; also S on right thigh; both hind feet white; medium size. One red and white speckled horse, medium size, branded PL combined (blotched) on right shoulder. One bay-roan horse, medium size, three white feet, branded fresh B C over a dash on left thigh. One brown horse about 15 hands high, branded fresh A with a curve over it on left shoulder and LHK combined on left thigh. One roan sorrel horse, medium size, bald face and four white feet; no brands. Two irongray horses, medium size; no brands. One light sorrel horse, medium size, branded tomahawk on both shoulders and E with a curve over it on left thigh. One bright bay horse, medium size; no brands. One bay roan, medium size, branded fresh R on right flank. One dark bay mare, about 15 hands high, branded x7 and diamond on left shoulder, and diamond S on left thigh. One light sorrel mare about 15 hands high, branded L on left shoulder and A on left flank; hind feet white. One dun horse, small size; dim T on left shoulder. One chestnut sorrel mare, small size, hind foot white, strip in face; branded a square with a semi-circle over it on left shoulder. One small bright bay mare, hind feet white; fresh branded a square with a semi-circle at the top on left shoulder, over dim brand. One small dark dun mare, black mane and tail, three white legs; branded dim J V on left shoulder and fresh B C over a dash on left thigh, and q combined on right shoulder. One small bright bay mare branded cross on left thigh; has sorrel mare colt. One small light roan horse, front feet white; branded U D on left shoulder and U D above a dash on left thigh—fresh. One small sorrel horse, light mane and tail; branded fresh U D on left shoulder and U D above a dash on left thigh. One small roan horse, three white feet; no brands.

Owners will please call, prove property, pay charges, and take their animals away.

September 11, 1884, notice of stock recovered from lynched horse thieves.

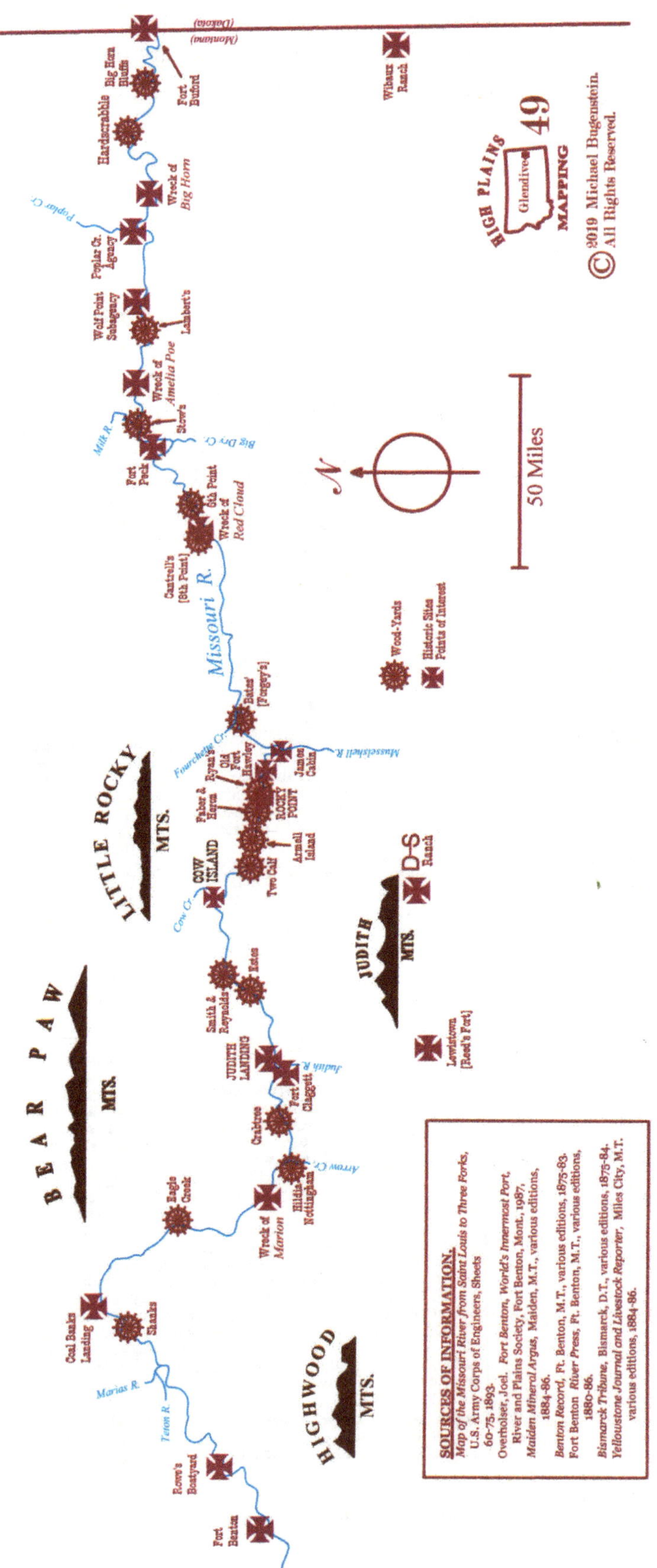

Along the Missouri River, an 1884 Montana "No Man's Land."

The *Rocky Mountain Husbandman* in White Sulphur Springs, Montana, reported the tally on August 21, 1884: "18 in all." But the spate of vigilante action was not quite complete.

From eastern Montana came sporadic reports, rumors really, of continuing activity. On August 16, 1884, the *Glendive Times* contained a report of two men lynched on the Little Missouri River. Another account from the Miles City *Yellowstone Journal* of September 13, 1884, reads:

Lynching Horse Thieves.

A correct version of the surrender of five horse thieves is given in the Glendive Times as follow: "Mr. Anderson, foreman for Granville Stuart, in charge of seven cow boys left Poplar Creek with five horse thieves, which they were taking to Meagher county. 'Flopping Bill' [Cantrell, a wood yard operator turned stock inspector], acting deputy sheriff, accompanied them as an officer in charge. At the Big Dry they were met at night by fifteen cow boys who enticed the officers and Mr. Anderson away from their camp, and at the muzzles of their revolvers took the horse thieves from the cow boys guarding them. Flopping Bill's dispatch says 'they didn't know what became of them,' but thinks there is little doubt but they are enjoying warmer weather than the rest of us. The hanging took place about five days ago.

News of the horse-thief clean-up was carried far and wide. The October 6, 1884, edition of the St. Paul (Minn.) *Daily Globe* carried a telegram from Glendive announcing the arrest of five suspected horse thieves at a ranch near present-day Sidney, Montana: "Whether these men are horse thieves or not remains for the court to decide, but it is certain they were arrested as such."

The 1884 Montana vigilante season concluded in October. The *Glendive Times* carried this item on October 25:

MILES CITY, Mont., Special Telegram, Oct. 20.—The fight at Mingusville [now Wibaux] between cowboys and horse thieves must have been a hot one. A report reaches here that five empty cowboys' saddles were found on the field. The cowboy vigilantes are said to have come from Wyoming. If so they are bent on vengeance, and the four that were hanged on Beaver [Creek] , seventeen miles north of Mingusville, near the Wibaux ranch, are part of their prey. . . .

On a final, grisly note, the *Yellowstone Journal* observed on November 29, 1884:

Mr. Lewis Nado, who recently returned from the Musselshell, reports that he and some of his companions found two skeletons lying on the ground about twelve miles from the mouth of the river, whilst, further on, the remains of a man was discovered, dangling from a tree. . . . The general impression that the several remains of the party in question formed part of the gang of horse and cattle thieves who were hanged by the vigilantes, last summer. Reports have been recently promulgated to the end that about the middle of the present month four men were lynched near Fort Buford for having stolen horses and cattle.

Horse thievery was by no means confined to Montana. The *River Press* published accounts of pitched battles between ranchers and horse thieves across the "Medicine Line," the border between the United States and the "British Possessions." It was also widespread in Wyoming and other parts of the west.

In Montana, the territorial legislature was controlled by the mining interests (cutthroats themselves) around Butte. While the importance of the ranching industry was undisputed, east of the Rockies was largely regarded as a no-mans-land. In Wyoming, the role of the legislature was to do the bidding of the Wyoming Stockgrowers' Association. In Montana the Association could and did exert political influence, but in Wyoming, the Stockgrowers' voice carried the rule of law.

A main issue was the branding of "mavericks," unbranded calves not in the direct company of their mothers. The bylaws of the Montana Stockgrowers' Association had a provision whereby ranch hands were allowed to apply their brand to legitimately lost livestock. The Wyoming Association, mostly comprised of eastern and foreign livestock syndicates, forbade this—mavericks had to be turned over to members of the Stockgrowers' Association and sold at auction. As may be imagined, this created hard feelings on both sides.

Additionally, Wyoming's very geography largely precluded settlement. Initially carved into five huge parallel north-to-south counties (Laramie, Albany, Carbon, Sweetwater, and Uinta), virtually the entire state, in areas distant from the Union Pacific railway corridor, were almost totally devoid of towns and villages. Only a few scattered stores and trading posts that catered to the local population. The cattle barons had the place to themselves, and they planned to keep it that way.

Horseflesh had the same value in Wyoming as any other place in the American West, and horse thievery was aggressively suppressed. Although every case was a little different, there was a predicable reaction. On March 1, 1884, the *Carbon County Journal*, in Rawlins, Wyoming, carried a fairly lengthy account where a Benjamin Twistleton used his earnings for constructing the school house at the Shoshone Agency to legally acquire about thirty horses. Two of his coworkers, G.E. (Yellowstone Bill) Rogers and Henry Leeper, relieved him of his purchase, and headed northward. Twistleton had an idea of who they were and where they were going. On January 28, he pursued the horse thieves to the No Water Ranch on the Big Horn River, where:

> . . . . At the time he overhauled them they had their horses picketed in a safe place and were making a fire. Twistleton rode up nearly to them and commanded them to "throw up your hands." They saw who it was and both jumped and grabbed their rifles, and Twistleton, who was now about thirty feet distant, shot Rogers dead, spending a bullet through his brain. As Rogers fell, he destroyed Leeper's aim, as the latter fired, and the ball whistled harmlessly past Twistleton's head. Twistleton fired instantly and shot Leeper in the abdomen, the bullet going clear through his body. Leeper cried out "My God, Ben I'll surrender."

> Twistleton jumped from his horse, and lifting the dying Leeper up, cared for him as best he could to relieve the death agony for nearly two hours until the grim angel came to his relief. Twistleton then went to the ranch near by and procured the services of E.R. Dunham, Clay Anderson, John Watts, and Dan Colson, who returned with him to the scene of the tragedy and decently buried the bodies of the two horse thieves. . . .

> Twistleton immediately returned to the agency, taking the stolen horses with him, and arrived there February 15. He collected evidence regarding the avowed intention of the

two man he killed, to steal his horses, and on Monday, February 18, went to North Fork and gave himself up to Justice of the Peace Cottrell, was arraigned and put under bail, pending judicial investigation of the affair. The general sentiment at Shoshone agency, where all the parties are known, is strongly in favor of Twistleton, and his discharge from custody is confidently expected.

(An example of a citizen initially taking the law in his own hands, expecting his eventual legal exoneration.)

An example of the widespread geographical nature of the horse thievery black market, along with the convoluted Territorial legal system, can be ascertained from this item that appeared in the April 24, 1886, *Carbon County Journal*:

> William Cummins, the horse thief brought in a few days ago from the north, is a wide range "rustler," being both a Nevada and Wyoming "rustler." Last spring a gang headed by one Andy Byers, stole two hundred horses in the Humboldt valley, Nevada, on the Elko ranges. The stock was divided into several bands , and pushed for Montana, Wyoming, and Dakota. Some have been heard of in Montana—others sold last summer in Spearfish, Dakota, while Byers and Cummins brought eighty [unintelligible] to this region, locating on the Stinking Water (in northern Wyoming) for the winter. Last December the men gathered up a [rail] car load of the horses for shipment to Ellendale [in present-day eastern North Dakota], where John Byers, a brother of Andy's, had a large farm. With this car load were taken several head stolen from John Chapman, the prominent Stinking Water horse raiser. Early last month, Chapman heard of his horses, and started after them. Arriving at Ellendale, he found two of his horses on the Byers' farm. Procuring requisition papers, he had both Byers boys and Cummins arrested. Through some flaw in the papers, the prisoners were released at Junction, Dakota, on a habeas corpus writ. The Byers boys at once fled. Correcting his papers, Chapman followed them. A friend of Chapman's named Cook arrested him [Cummins] on his own authority, and took him to Billings, Montana. Here Chapman could not be found, and Cummins was again released. Cook now swore out a warrant against the escaping thief on an old charge of saddle stealing, and lodged him in the Billings jail. Chapman soon appeared and the slippery prisoner is now in the Lander [Wyo.] jail.

(It should be noted that the shortest present-day distance from Elko, Nevada to Ellendale, North Dakota, is just under 1,200 miles—quite a journey on the various 1886 means of transportation. It can be safely assumed that rancher Chapman would have rather be using his horses than chasing them all over "hell-and-gone.")

Things in Wyoming continued in this vein, the cattle syndicates using the government land as their own private fiefdom. Any attempts for small operators to intrude were ruthlessly suppressed. It was a hard place for an honest man to make an honest living.

In the summer of 1889, two upright settlers, Jim Averill and his wife, Ella Watson, proved up on a legitimate homestead in the Sweetwater valley in central Wyoming, where they legally acquired a few cattle and ran a small store. Their fenced acreage happened to occupy the pasture of a large self-proclaimed cattle baron. On July 20, he and a few other local cattlemen kidnapped Jim and Ella and hanged them to a tree, for no other reason than the ranchmen wanted them out of the way. A local

Paying the Fiddler, by Charles M. Russell (1919). Courtesy of C.M. Russell Museum, Great Falls, MT.

account can be found in the *Bessemer Wyoming Journal* on August 1, 1889. The resulting uproar was white-washed in the Cheyenne newspapers at the bidding of the stockgrowers. Over the course of a century, the event remained a forbidden subject, until 1993, when George W. Hufsmith described the whole dirty deal in his exposé, *The Wyoming Lynching of Cattle Kate 1889*.

(Another classic study of western lynch law can be found in Walter van Tilburg Clark's perceptive 1940 work, *The Ox-Bow Incident*.)

Extra-legal activity continued in Wyoming even after statehood in 1890. A rancher, suspected of complicity in the horse-thief industry, was taken from his home near Newcastle and hanged to a tree several miles away. The June 19, 1891, edition of The *Newcastle Journal* carried a lengthy account of the incident under the banner headline:

The Newcastle Journal.

NEWCASTLE, WESTON COUNTY, WYO., FRIDAY, JUNE 19, 1891.

Tom Waggoner Hanged!

By a Party of Unknown Men Claiming to be Sheriffs from Sundance.

The Body Found Three Miles From the Ranch After It Had Been Hanging Ten Days.

No Clue to the Identity of the Members of the Lynching Party Has Been Found.

The article goes on in great detail about the particulars of the event and subsequent inquest, including a graphic description of a man's body after he had been hanging for ten days in the summer sun, which will not be given here.

Finally, in 1892, matters came to a head near Buffalo, Wyoming. The "Johnson County War" brought the intervention of the United States Army to quell the disturbance. Finally, some semblance of law and order was established on the ranges of Wyoming. (Rather than continuing on this tangent, a detailed account, *The War on Powder River,* by Dorothy S. Johnson, is recommended.)

After Montana statehood in 1889, horse theft continued to be a problem on the range, but the system of state courts was relied on to deal with it. As the frontier began to settle up, new counties and judicial districts were created, increasing access to the legal system. Horse thievery cases continued to be on the docket, however.

In April of 1892, a large band of horses were stolen from their range in the Sweet Grass Hills of Northern Montana. After a dogged pursuit of over eight hundred miles, a Havre dispatch was carried in the July 30, 1892, edition of the *Great Falls Weekly Tribune:*

WEEKLY TRIBUNE.

GREAT FALLS, MONTANA, SATURDAY MORNING, JULY 30, 1892.

HORSE THIEVES CAPTURED.

Hoit and Spaulding Captured in Northern Minnesota.

HAVRE, Mont., July 22.—[Special to the TRIBUNE.]—The two horse thieves, Fred Hoit and William Spaulding, who stole 150 fine horses from the range in Sweet Grass hills last April, have been run down and captured by the vigorous pursuit and ingenuity of Charles Hawley who has been on their trail for six weeks.

The horse thieves were caught in northern Minnesota while attending a country dance.

Hoit was visiting relatives in the town. About 100 of the horses have been recovered, the remainder were sold all along the line of the Great Northern R. R., from Havre to Minot. Sam Herron, stock inspector, took these men from here yesterday to Fort Benton, Mont. They are the same two men who were acquitted at Benton last March of poisoning a team of horses in the Little Rocky mountains. Twelve hundred dollars was found in their possession when captured. Spaulding is a notorious tough and a bad man, and Choteau county will surely fix them at least for the next twenty years.

Northern Montana continued to be a lawless frontier. A short item was published in Fort Benton on July 20, 1892:

THE RIVER PRESS.

Fort Benton, Montana, Wednesday, July 20, 1892.

Glasgow News: Horse rustlers have been making a successful raid through North Dawson county, thirty-five head having been run off their range between Glasgow and Saco. Dan Miller is the heaviest loser as his band consisted of twenty two head of well-bred, big animals. These were taken from the vicinity of Tampico. The thieves have evidently gotten well out of the country, as the searchers have been unable to come up with them, although they have ridden hard for five days.

Other Montana ranges were similarly afflicted. Other horse thieves were actively working the ranges around Red Lodge, Montana, southwest of Billings. Under the headline "The Gang Captured," the *Red Lodge Picket* continued on July 22, 1893:

> . . . Anthony and William Chaffin missed twenty head of their horses about a month ago and in looking for them they found that a bunch answering to their had been seen and were being driven east by four men. Telegrams were sent to different points along the railway and last week L.P. Sichler, of this place, In company of Under Sheriff Ramsey, of Yellowstone county and stock inspector Billy Smith of Miles City in pursuit. They overtook all of them and their horses with the exception of Sharples [an alleged member of the gang] at Sentinel Butte near the Dakota line. At first the men could not be found but finally in an old cellar under a stable they were discovered. Upon being ordered to come out they refused to comply and it was only after a few shots were fired into the roof of the cellar that they appeared and held up their hands for surrender. They were taken to Billings and lodged in jail and the horses were left to feed for about a week so they could stand the drive back. . . .

In September, 1893, the *Picket* announced that the perpetrators had been sentenced to seven years in prison.

Throughout the 1890s, newcomers continued to filter onto the northern grasslands to try their hand at ranching. With the completion of the Great Northern Railroad, transporting cattle to the markets in Chicago or St. Paul was no longer a problem. Ranchers continued to "prove up" on homestead patents, generally around springs or creeks. Along with ranchers came fences, mostly to protect hayfields, which impeded the free migration of livestock. The Northern Plains were beginning to be "settled up."

As the curtain closed on the Western frontier, horse-thief operations became more and more remote, until their operations were scattered far into the hinterlands, away from the "long arm of the law." In November, 1898, a small item appeared in the *Valley County Gazette* in Glasgow, Montana:

SATURDAY, NOV. 5, 1898.

T. L. Blackman, general manager of the Home Land & Cattle company, was a visitor in Glasgow a few days the first of the week. He informs us that a gang of horse thieves located at the mouth of the Big Dry all this summer, recently entered the company's pasture at Pearmond and during the night when a heavy storm was raging, drove off thirty-five head of fine saddle horses. A reward for the apprehension of the thieves has been offered.

The horse-thief market faded over time. In spite of the shrinking free range, organized horse theft remained a problem as long as horses retained their usefulness, which remained well into the 1900s.

But times were changing. Around 1905, railroads began extensively advertising free lands open for settlement. A deluge of promotional literature was distributed in the fertile states of the Midwest and in Europe, where vestiges of the feudal system remained. If a princely 20-acre farm could be cleared in Indiana, just imagine what could be done with 160 acres in Montana! And why stay in Europe with your destiny determined by birth when the U.S. Government was giving away land for free? With these ideas in mind, tens of thousands of land-seekers flooded the arid plains.

The Homestead Era created a new demand for work horses. By this time, horses were not primarily used for stock-growing operations, but rather for farming. In addition to riding the range, horses were a necessity for pulling a plow, and thousands upon thousands were used in this manner. Horses markets were set up in towns of any size and did a brisk business. Some of these horses were undoubtedly stolen.

Other forces were diminishing the market. After 1900, mechanization began to infiltrate the northern plains as extensive farming took hold. Tractors and threshers began to be utilized between neighbors to take care of back-breaking tasks. Horses were retained to perform day-to-day farm chores. Additionally, and importantly, automobiles were found to be a convenient, if balky, means of transportation, albeit on bad roads.

In the early 1920s the horse market collapsed. There was a glut on the market as discouraged homesteaders gave up and departed, first trying to give their horses away, then simply turning them loose to fend for themselves. It was no longer necessary to buy horses, stolen or otherwise, when it was possible to ride into the badlands and rope all that were needed.

The final nail for the horse-thief trade came in the post-World War II era, when wide-spread prosperity enabled farmers to buy farm machinery, which was expensive but obtainable. The need for horses evaporated as the northern ranges entered the modern era.

LATER . . . IN NORTH DAKOTA — 6

After the Natives were isolated on their reservations, the Northern Plains were opened for settlement. Immediately railroad building began, followed on its heels by a steady stream of land seekers, storekeepers, saloons, and various tradesmen.

The Northern Pacific Railroad began building west from the Red River Valley in the early 1870s. A land-grant railroad, United States government awarded the N.P. checkerboard sections for forty miles on either side of the track for opening up the country to homesteading. In 1871 and 1872, the N.P. began to survey its proposed western route through contested tribal lands, protected by the U.S. Army. Actual construction continued until the rails reached Bismarck when the Panic of 1873 halted progress "dead in its tracks."

There things remained until 1879 when the tribes had been subdued and market conditions improved. Construction resumed westward, but presented new challenges on the often-rugged sedimentary plains. In 1880, accompanied by a military escort, the road reached the badlands of the Little Missouri River. After laying a twisting, curving track in over the treeless prairie, the rails arrived in the rude settlement of Glendive, Montana Territory, in July of 1881, thence following Yellowstone River grade to Livingston for the next 340 miles. In the fall of 1883, the N.P. met its tracks built eastward from the coast at the hamlet of Gold Creek, Montana. Representatives of the Crow tribe, as allies of the United States Government, participated in the golden spike ceremony.

The "Manitoba Road" (renamed the Great Northern Railroad in 1890) was laid for over 600 miles from Minot, Dakota Territory, across the former tribal hunting ground, to Helena, Montana, in 1887. Strung along the track, every six miles or so, were a series of stations: a siding for meeting trains, a section house for maintenance-of-way employees (some contained a telegrapher's office), and a water tank for steam locomotives. (Interestingly, most of these stations were said to have been named by a railroad official spinning a globe at the main office in St. Paul.) At some of these stations, substantial towns and villages sprang up—for instance, Glasgow (site of a round house), Malta, Harlem, and Chinook, Montana. Others remained merely railroad outposts: Ashfield, Exeter, Eureka, and North Fork, virtually forgotten today.

As the 1890s progressed, the Northern Plains began to settle up in earnest. The Great Northern, not being a land-grant railroad, had a particular interest in settling the country. In Montana, moving large amounts of livestock and farm commodities was next to impossible without railroads. The newly-minted settlements provided a source for supplies, schooling, social life, and church. Instead of roving bachelor cowboys, the plains began to attract families. Not only did it connect cities, it also focused great, and often exaggerated, efforts to attract local customers along its route. Stockyards and grain elevators were built at almost all the stations along the line. Hundreds of thousands of cattle were shipped to the Midwest annually.

The Posse, by Charles M. Russell (1895). Image courtesy of Amon Carter Museum, Fort Worth, TX.

However, the nefarious element never really evacuated the northern plains either. There were still plenty of isolated spaces in which to operate away from the prying eyes of citizens and the law. But after a while, new settlers began to locate ranches at springs and watercourses farther from the main line. This pushed the outlaws deeper into the hinterlands, so by 1900 or so, their haunts were mainly around the isolated Little Rocky Mountains, the Canadian border, and in the still-wild country near the Little Missouri River in western North Dakota.

Nearing the 20th century, newly established counties began building roads, albeit primitive, that connected the county seats with remote areas that had been virtual wilderness just a few years before. Replacing old trails, the new roads allowed increased settlement, which were at that time mostly small ranch operations. There was still very little large-scale farming on the Northern Plains.

About this time, U.S. Government surveyors became a larger presence on the plains. Although surveying had been taking place for decades, it was mostly along the railroad or military corridors, with some exceptions. Around the turn of the 20th century, they began working their way into the interior. This enabled settlers to file for homesteads using legal descriptions of their land: section, township, and range. Within a few years, depending on the type of claim, they could own their land outright. (Former pre-emption claims could be patented as well, using a different description.)

The "border outlaws" tried to operate in the shrinking sphere. Horse stealing continued, but the range of the trade was diminishing. However, many of the horse thieves diversified into cattle rustling. Rustling cattle was slow and somewhat geographically limited, and a whole lot less glamorous than horse-stealing, but it could also be a good source of income, at least for a while.

Rustlers would obtain range cattle and bring them to co-operating ranchers who didn't care much about pedigree. From there, the ranchers would sell them to area butcher shops, where the finished beef would be marketed to the locals as the growing towns and settlements brought a fresh demand for beef. The arrangement worked well for everyone except the legitimate owners.

In 1900, horse-thief gangs still operated on the closing frontier, on a smaller scale. One of these had their headquarters near Bennie Peer Creek in far-western North Dakota, about twenty miles east of the old Tokna Dunlap place near present-day Savage, Montana. Somewhat a local concern, they bedeviled area ranchers by relieving them of their horses and cattle and then marketing them in turn.

Their purported leader was Jim McPeak, who also went by Jack McCarty. A Missouri native, he is thought to have drifted northward in the late 1870s at the dawn of the ranching era. He seems to have spent his time drifting between the ranges around Glendive and Dickinson. By the 1890s, he had gained a reputation as a competent cowhand. His is rumored to have been involved in a disturbance in Richardton, North Dakota, in about 1899. He is also reported to have escaped from Stock Inspector Billy Smith in Fallon, Montana, in 1900. Brash and boastful, he vowed that he would never be taken alive. When he located on a tributary of Bennie Peer Creek, not far from a 101 Ranch cow camp (part of a Chicago syndicate), is not known.

One of McPeak's targets was James McEwen (Mac) Uhlman, proprietor of the Morning Star Cattle Company. The operation was established across the Missouri River a little downstream from Williston, North Dakota, in 1891, running the distinctive "Bird-Head" brand. A steady, well-maintained operation, by 1901 the Bird-Head was an important ranching hub, shipping cattle and horses over the Great Northern Railroad.

The circle began to tighten around McPeak in January, 1901, when an associate named Walter Barnett was arrested while attempting to ship a train car of horses from Sentinel Butte, North Dakota, to a buyer in Iowa. Two area ranchers identified their horses as being their own. Additionally, the bill of sale for the horses was found to have the signatures for both the seller and the buyer in the same handwriting. Barnett was bound over for trial before the Stark County District Court in April.

McPeak's operations continued throughout eastern Montana and western North Dakota. In early spring of 1901, he is believed to have stolen horses in Glendive, Montana, and over thirty head of cattle from Mac Uhlman's ranch south of Williston.

In early April, 1901, having heard of McPeak's rumored whereabouts, newly elected Stark County Sheriff John Goodall organized a posse which included the sheriffs of Billings County, North Dakota, and Dawson County, Montana; two Montana stock inspectors, George Twible and Billy Smith; the legally deputized Mac Uhlman; and a few others. On April 6 they rode northward from Wibaux, Montana.

After riding for over 60 miles, on the following afternoon, they arrived at the Leakey, McDonald, and Clark ranch, located about three miles east of the state line. The posse immediately arrested "Long John" Leakey and John McDonald, wanted for cattle-stealing, and waited for their leader.

Jim McPeak rode up to the ranch about 6 o'clock in the afternoon on April 7. Sensing something amiss, he turned his horse, bearing Glendive rancher J.S. Day's TD brand, and galloped toward a nearby

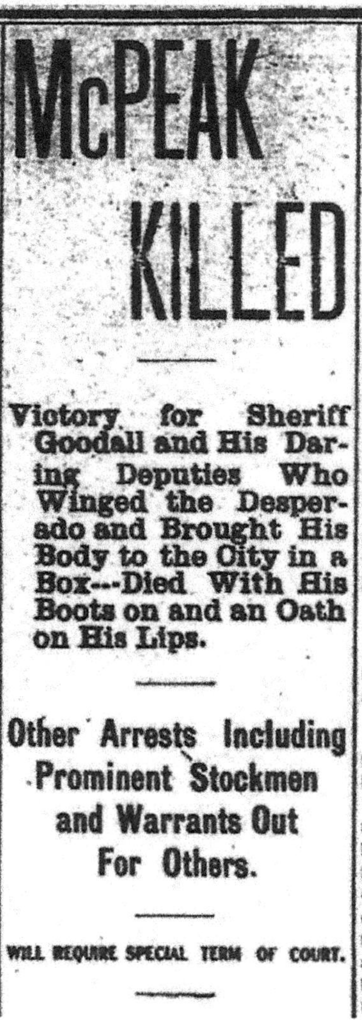

Banner headline from April 13, 1901, announcing the demise of Jim McPeak.

cut bank for protection. Ordered to surrender, he rode on, until the posse fired in unison. McPeak's TD horse absorbed fifteen or twenty bullets, while McPeak absorbed only one, through his body above his heart. He was carried to the ranch house, where he died about ten hours later, swearing at the posse members the entire time.

Recovered nearby were 22 head of cattle bearing the "Bird-Head" brand, along with eleven hides. Nine horses were also in the small herd branded +S from Glendive, altered to HES.

McDonald was brought to Dickinson, "Long John" having escaped shortly after his capture.

View of 101 Ranch where Jim McPeak was cornered, from Bird-Head
Ranch memoirs.

As McPeak was meeting his demise, his partner, Barnett, learned his fate at the court house. He was found guilty of cattle theft and sentenced to four years. He used the time learning to make bricks. John McDonald, formerly a Wibaux sheriff's deputy, was held for trial. In July he escaped, rode 90 miles, and was recaptured. The final outcome of the case cannot be determined; the records seem to have been lost.

Soon the whole conspiracy unraveled. It seemed that McPeak and his associates were providing stolen cattle to a rancher south of Wibaux, who in turn sold them to butcher shops around eastern Montana. The rancher, who will remain anonymous, was shortly released on a writ of *habeas corpus*.

(Glendive, Montana, was somewhat regarded as a hub for the horse thief trade. A well-to-do area on the city's north side continues to be known as "Horse Thief Row.")

The days of brazen, large-scale horse thievery were severely numbered. Around 1899, surveyors from the Government Land Office began measuring off the remaining flatlands of the Northern Plains. On their heels followed thousands upon thousands of homesteaders lured to the unforgiving climate by the U.S. Government and the railroads eager to sell their land grants, in a scheme that Walt Coburn termed the "Big Swindle." Along with homesteaders came fences. The new farmers shredded the native soil. Thereafter, virtually every quarter-section was occupied by hopeful, but largely clueless, small Midwestern farmers doomed to lives of hardship and deprivation. Their farm animals suffered with them. After decades of untold misery, the federal government, under the "New Deal," came up with a plan of western resettlement as part of the Agricultural Adjustment Act.

As the 20th century progressed, horse-thief operations were driven toward the international border, their final haven. By 1905, true "border outlaws" were squeezed along the boundary. Noteworthy among this gentry was "Dutch Henry" Ieuch (or Jeuch) who had been a denizen around Saco, Montana, where his I-B brand was registered in 1892. As the Milk River area was settled up, he moved his enterprise to the vicinity of present-day Plentywood, Montana. It is believed that he met his violent demise around 1904.

lench & Botsford, Saco, Dawson county. Brand for cattle, thus, on left ribs. Vent for cattle, same, on left hip.

Listing of "Dutch Henry's" brand from 1892 Montana state brand book.

Organized gangs were run out of business, but small-scale cattle and horse theft would continue, human nature being what it is. In 1920, the Eighteenth Amendment proclaimed Prohibition. Immediately, the criminal element had found a new way to ply their trade. By the time the Midwestern gangs came of age in the 1930s, horses were no longer their means of transportation. They now rode Fords, Essexes, and Terraplanes.

EPILOGUE: WILD AGAIN

Horses and humans have a complex and symbiotic relationship. Horses look to humans for kindness, sustenance, safety, and leadership, in return for a hard day's work. Humans look for brute strength, instinctive savvy, companionship, and possibly prestige, in exchange for filling the basic needs of their charges.

The above *quid pro quo* is an oversimplification. Horses, like humans, possess a spectrum of dispositions. Horses can be loyal, hardworking, playful, or affectionate. They can also be lazy, obstinate, surly, mean, and big enough to be dangerous. Human beings can be the same. Many times a horse and rider will mirror the emotions of one another and blend into a cohesive unit; other times the relationship just won't work.

The two species also possess a love of freedom. Originally, both were wild animals, and over time, a socialization transpired where both learned to live exclusively among its own kind. Although millions of years apart, people and horses, in many ways, evolved on a somewhat parallel path.

In the 1870s, white immigrants were making noticeable inroads into the western wilderness, and European influence was starting to be felt in the land. But no matter how many railroads, trails, telegraph lines, mines and lumber mills, towns and settlements, farms, ranches, and solitary cabins dotted the landscape, there was still plenty of empty space left for deer, elk, moose, antelope, beaver, and mink, with predators such as coyotes, bobcats, cougars, and bears to keep them in check. Over time, the human presence became larger and larger, until at some point, *homo sapiens* became the apex species.

In the early American West, horses had the space to exist far from the human sphere. These horses, thousands of them, had escaped as the tribes were confined and the mining camps moved (or had decided on their own that ranch life was not their cup of tea). Undoubtedly, there were others that had roamed the sagebrush range ever since they were liberated by the Pueblo Revolt.

Although wild horses roamed all over the west, they were especially numerous in the arid Great Basin province of Nevada and Utah. There, prospectors congregated primarily in mining camps which were seemingly innumerable but geographically compact. The pioneer ranching industry tried to establish a toe-hold, but the range was overgrazed by the 1880s and essentially ruined. The remaining marginal grasslands could support few ranchers. Barbed wire fences were not frequently seen on the parched landscape.

Wild horses from far and wide found their way into the harsh environment, keeping their distance from their main competitor, the encroaching human being. There they grazed, cavorted, ran free, fought, reproduced, and often starved, seemingly protected in the wide-open spaces on unfenced government land.

By the 1890s, the ever-increasing number of wild horses was starting to attract the attention of the ranchers who regarded them as pests. Newspapers articles began to appear of cowboys trying to corral the beasts, a test of horsemanship that would hopefully ease stress on the sparse range.

On December 25, 1890, a newspaper in Battle Mountain reported on conditions on the range:

CENTRAL NEVADAN.

Vol 6   BATTLE MOUNTAIN, NEVADA, THURSDAY, DECEMBER 25 1890   No 51.

Warner Hillyer, of Antelope Valley, who was in town during the week, reports thousands of wild horse ranging on the high mountain plateaus near his home. He states that it is almost impossible to raise a band of tame animal in that section as they soon find their way into the wild habitation of the mustang.

The *Iron County News*, published in Cedar City, Utah, carried this item on January 24, 1891:

Iron County News.

VOL. I.   CEDAR CITY, UTAH, JANUARY 24, 1891.   NO. 9

There are a great many wild, unbroken horses runing at large on the desert between Iron Co and Pioche. These animals are generally the colts of horse stock turned out on the range by Iron county people. Now the question is who has the right to dispose of the stock? Can those parties having branded horses running on the desert say that the boys who shall drive up this stock can have all the unbranded horses for their trouble? This would be perfectly ligitimate if the stock be proven to belong to the parties disposing of it. But perhaps there others be-ides Iron Co. people who are interested in these wild horses. The stock needs looki g after badly, for they are a nuisance at pres nt. and are occupying one of the be t winter ranges in Utah to the exclusion of other more valuable stock.

On February 27, 1892, the *Eureka Weekly Sentinel* in Nevada carried this article about cowboys going after a herd of wild horses that had gathered in Lander County:

EUREKA WEEKLY SENTINEL.

VOLUME XII.   EUREKA, NEVADA, SATURDAY, FEBRUARY 27, 1892.   NUMBER 26.

Hunting Wild Horses.

The Austin Advocate says: Bar Francis, John Cadra and James Murphy are getting ready to go to Antelope range, 40 miles northwest of Austin, and try the scheme of catching some of the untamed wild horses in that country. They think that the snow being deep and the animals poor and weak from the long spell of cold weather, that they may be able to catch some horses that cannot be caught in the Spring, Summer or Fall. We wish them good luck, and would be glad if every mustang in Nevada could be captured and sold out of the State or put to work. The fewer we have the better off the State will be.

While ranchers largely regarded wild horses as a pest, many cowboys harbored a grudging respect for the beasts. The September 22, 1892, issue of *The Central Nevadan* featured a report of wild horses protecting their herd against a pack of wolves. Another colorful account, which appeared in the *Lyon County Times* of Dayton, Nevada, on April 28, 1894, carried details of a thrilling chase under the title of **CORRELING WILD HORSES**. These accounts are worthy of publication and are presented as separate illustrations.

An important article appeared in the November 21, 1894, edition of *The Salt Lake Herald,* entitled: **DRUG ON THE MARKET. Horses Are Worth Less Than Five Dollars a Head.** Several pertinent points were brought up, and it was estimated that there were *two hundred thousand* wild horses devouring the Nevada range:

> . . . It is very evident that the day of high-priced horseflesh—except that classified as thoroughbred—has gone. Electric cars, railroads and bicycles have played havoc with the general market. . . .
>
> Most of the wild horses are in the neighborhood of Elko and Iron Point. A few years ago, there was turned loose from the Evans ranche [sic], near Iron Point, a fine thoroughbred stallion. He joined the neighboring bands of wild horses and could not be got back again.

The result was that the quality of the herds was greatly improved. He left many colts that were much superior to the old stock. The various bands have much increased since then. While many of the horses would not be called first class, are very fine, and all are as tough as pine knots, and as fleet as there is any use in having horses.

They are eating the grass off, and making it hard picking in places for cattle and sheep, and as the ranchers cannot catch the wild horses, they are shooting themdown whenever they get sight of them and can get up close enough. The latter is not always an easy task. In fact it is usually a most difficult thing to do. . . .

Supply being more than adequate, the price of horses continued to plummet. On November 13, 1895, the Elko *Daily Independent* reported a herd of wild horses brought to Lovelock, Nevada, brought *seven cents a head.*

The *Elko Independent* reported on May 2, 1897:

Weekly Independent.

VOLUME XXXI.   ELKO, NEVADA, SUNDAY, MAY 2, 1897.   NUMBER 18.

Wild Horses.

A large band of wild horses is browsing near Aurora, Esmeralda county. It numbers several hundred. A spavined old animal that can hardly stand in harness becomes as nimble as a colt shortly after it has joined the band, which is composed of horses and mules that have been enticed away from ranches in the valley. They are wilder than mustangs born on the plains, roaming up and down the slope for several hundred miles. There are many good animals among them. The leader, the king of the herd, is said to be a magnificent buckskin stallion with black points, who is always in the lead and ready to fight anything that intrudes upon his harem.

CENTRAL NEVADAN.

Vol. 8.   BATTLE MOUNTAIN, NEVADA, THURSDAY, SEPTEMBER 22, 1892.   No. 27.

A BRAVE BATTLE.

In the southern part of Nevada, especially in Nye county, there are many bands of wild mustangs. For steady running nothing of the equine breed can equal the wild horse, and as a mountain climber he is scarcely excelled by the goat. Three hunters in the mountains recently fell afoul of a band of forty of these mustangs under peculiar circumstances. The three men were in camp, and just about to turn in, when they heard a roar like the tread of an advancing army. In the dim light they could see nothing, but as the noise approached the three men stood on guard. In another minute a band of mustangs emerged from a stretch of pines, running at a fearful rate, their nostrils dilated and their long manes and tails flying in the wind. On they came stright for the camp. "We saw we were to be ground under their heels unless we did something," says the narrator, "and we began to shout and halloo like mad. Our horses were meantime dashing and charging, and it looked as if every instant they would break away. We grasped our guns and fired over the heads of the horses, for they were so handsome that we didn't want to kill them. Finally, just at the last second of time, when we thought we were to be borne down by the wild throng, they turned and dashed down the hill into the darkness. By this time we began to hear weird howls and neighing and stamping. Every once in a while we heard a whack, as though something was hitting something else with terrific force, combined with louder howls. The noise was just behind the spur of pine trees, a quarter of a mile away. It continued louder than ever, and two of us concluded to push on out and see what the rumpus was. Judge of our surprise when we saw three old stallions surrounded by a pack of big mountain wolves and kicking and biting at a furious rate. Three or four of the wolves had been sent to grass, their ribs broken and disabled in other ways. Around the stallions were the wolves, snapping and growling and showing their long white teeth. The horses stood almost head to head and planted terrific blows on the heads and bodies of the wolves. Every once in a while a wolf described a parabola in the air. It was a scene long to be remembered. Out there in the keen, crisp night air of the mountains the three wild horses were fighting not only for their lives but for the lives of the younger and weaker members of the band, who were being defended from the wolves. The hunters at once sided with the horses, and with several well directed volleys put the wolves to flight. Then with a neigh of joy, and perhaps of gratitude, the horses galloped away in the darkness, and the hunters returned to their campfire.—Gohlen Days.

Lyon County Times.

VOL. XXXV.   Dayton, Nevada, Saturday, April 28, 1894.   No. 17.

CORRELING WILD HORSES.

A Couple of Phillip's Vaqueros Run in a Band.

The first of last week Les. Douglass and Clarence Tailleur started from the old Buckland ranch with a drive of beef cattle for the Wadsworth market. When about six miles from that place they saw a bunch of horses off to the west of them, and Les thought he would go and take a look at them, but discovered they were very wild, and he could not get near them. The boys took the cattle to Wadsworth, and leaving that place early the next morning, thought they would round up the horses on their way back to the ranch. They found the band again all right, and then they separated, Les. going to the west and above the horses on the side hill to prevent them from crossing the ridge or getting into one of the numerous small and rocky canyons thereabouts, while Clarence came up behind and a little to the east so as to give the band a start down the hill towards Sand Valley, distant about eight miles. When the horses started they made for the top of the hill, and nearly succeeded in crossing owing to Les. meeting with an accident. In crossing a small canyon his stumbled and turned a complete somerset, throwing Les. about nine feet over his head. He lit in a sitting position and nearly knocked his brains out, but fortunately gained his feet in time to catch his horse. Mounting, he turned the band, and then they had a straight run to Sand Valley, where they rounded the horses up and found that only two of them were branded. Then the boys concluded to take them home, and continued on down Sand Valley and out onto the desert, where the horses made numerous breaks to get back into the hills. Les. was too quick for them and would turn them towards Clarence, and once the latter had a run of about three miles, and just as he headed the band off his horse stepped in a badger hole and fell flat on his side. Clarence was quick enough to throw his leg over the horn of the saddle and light on his feet, thereby saving himself an ugly fall and possibly a broken leg. But they got the horses under control and finally correled them, after a hard run of nineteen or twenty miles over rocks, sand and sagebrush. This band of horses is supposed to have sprung from the sci-sor brand band which used to run in the hills between Wadsworth and Fort Churchill a good many years ago. The boys think they have never been corraled before, as only two of them are branded, and they are highly elated over their feat.

As the problem worsened, wild horse roundups became frequent. Horses were driven down canyons flanking the mountain ranges and herded into makeshift corrals for sorting. The branded horses were returned to their owners, possible work horses were brought in, and the remainder were shot or sold for slaughter. In one such event, in 1895, 400 wild horses were captured near Pyramid Lake. Another account, from 1902, reported 600 head rounded up in the desolate Ione valley in central Nevada. On June 3, 1909, the Fort Benton *River Press* carried news of the "biggest wild horse hunt ever attempted in Nevada," consisting of 500 cowboys and covering fifty square miles north of Wadsworth. Round-ups persisted throughout the 20th century and still occasionally occur today, using different methods.

In 1897, the Nevada legislature passed a new law allowing local ranchers to apply to the county for permits to hunt wild horses. With too many horses covering too much area, the statute didn't do much good. It was repealed in 1905, another political controversy with no agreeable solution.

On the northern ranges, where the grass was still good, another dynamic was coming into play. Around 1905, hordes of deluded homesteaders began arriving to rip open the unbroken sod with the forlorn hope of producing crops like they could in the Midwest. Within a few short years, the prairie was altered from an ecosystem that had matured over millennia. Get-rich-quick schemes and half-baked science helped the newcomers rationalize their unsuitable farming techniques. With 12 inches of annual precipitation (5-7 inches in the critical spring months), give or take, farming conditions were vastly different from the land they had left behind. This was not considered—supposedly, "rain followed the plow."

Beasts of burden were essential to farm on the Northern Plains. Whether it be horses, oxen, or mules, farm animals provided the motive power to break through the spongy virgin soil. A good day's work was considered necessary to plow an acre of ground, only to find that the bounty of corn, squash, or truck vegetables could not be achieved without some sort of irrigation.

In the early homesteading years, the weather co-operated, mostly. But in the late 1910s the climate began to turn dry. Rainfall could no longer be relied upon for the water necessary for the germinating crops. The wind blew all the time, and soil, the source of their sustenance, would be transformed into dust that was carried miles into the air. In dry months (and years), grasshoppers devoured the fruits of hard labor. Good crops could be hailed out in a matter of minutes. The farmers, on their 160- or 320-acre homesteads, found themselves heartbroken and disillusioned. Yet they and their suffering families soldiered on—it was all they had. Still, most farmers managed to scrape out a meager existence. Even if they had nothing to sell, they could still generally grow enough to feed themselves.

Coincidentally, World War I also increased for the demand for horses, which the U.S. Army needed to move artillery. Great Plains horse ranchers, temporarily propped up, found themselves hard-pressed to meet the requirement, and auctioneers were kept busy. But after the 1918 Armistice, the war-horse industry collapsed.

Throughout the 1920s, the farm economy was stifled by bad economic policy and overextended credit. Farmers could not borrow against next year if there was no crop forthcoming. Undercapitalized rural banks failed by the hundreds.

In 1931, the weather became dryer yet. The Great Plains were in a full-fledged drought. Miles City, Montana, had a yearly total of just over six inches of precipitation; about 2.4 inches fell in the spring. Where small farmers had been faced with hunger before (itself an irony), now they were threatened with outright starvation. Their animals became gaunt and listless—there just was not enough for them to eat.

SECOND MONTHLY SALE

OF RANGE HORSES BY THE

Glendive Horse Sales Company

GLENDIVE, MONTANA.

We Sold No Horses Last Year But We Have the Cream of the Range Country to Sell At This Sale.

If You Have Any Horses, Cattle, or Sheep For Sale, List Them With Us.

Dates of This Sale
SEPTEMBER 1, 2 and 3.

Our Next and Last SALE for 1908, will be Oct. 1st, 2nd and 3rd.

1500 HEAD OF HORSES direct from the producers

Glendive Horse Sales Company,

CHAPPELL, Manager.   GLENDIVE, MONTANA.   GEO. M. BEASLEY, Secretary.
Auctioneer, Baird, Midway Horse Market, St. Paul, Minn.

An auction advertisement appeared in the *Yellowstone Monitor* in 1908 in Glendive, Montana, for the sale of domestic horses.

As the "Dirty Thirties" deepened, the long-suffering farmers had to face reality. Many of them made the hard decision to leave. And depart they did—dinner was left on the table, furniture stayed in the house, farm animals were set free to fend for themselves on the desiccated open range.

Wild horses had been considered a problem in eastern Montana since the mid-20s. Some of these horses, numbering about a *quarter of a million*, were descendants of horses undoubtedly running free since Territorial days, accompanied by escaped ranch horses, released homesteaders' horses, draft-dodging military horses, and any others who cared to join. Consuming what little marginal grassland which was left after the dry years, the wild horses became the focus of a widespread campaign of elimination.

In 1924, a disagreement arose between the Crow Tribe and local nontribal ranchers over grazing livestock. The ranchers, who held some grazing rights on the Reservation, regarded the tribally-controlled horses as interfering with their stockgrowing operations (a supreme irony). As a result of this dispute, the federal government authorized the slaughter of 44,000 "worthless and wild Indian ponies" on the Crow Reservation, ostensibly on tribal grasslands.

As range conditions deteriorated, local ranchers began conducting wild horse roundups in various districts around eastern Montana. On June 4, 1926, *The Havre Daily News Promoter* carried a brief item from the wide-open expanse in eastern Montana:

Wild Horses Being Removed From Range

Miles City, June 4.—Two wild horse roundups have been completed and another is drawing to a close in the territory between Circle, McCone county, and Parris and Purewater, Garfield county, according to Tom Browning.

The horses estimate to number about 15,000. A large number of the horses are destined to be shipped to Rockfield [Rockford], Ill., and Butte, Montana to the packing plants and will be converted into meat.

Wild horses were prevalent all over eastern Montana. South of Havre, ranchers in the Bear Paw foothills complained that

Hundreds of wild horses are running at large on the Beaver Creek National Park [a local recreation area], south of Havre, tearing down the fences of farms and playing havoc with crops, according to a delegation of ranchers, who attended the meeting of the city council last night in an effort to make some arrangements to police the park grounds.

Most of the horses, the ranchers say, were gathered in a roundup of abandoned horses under the state law last spring, but were not claimed by any owners and nor market could be found for them. Efforts were made to induce buyers to come here from various abattoirs but without success. After the horses had been advertised it was found impossible dispose of them they were turned loose.

Three months later, after the wild horse roundup south of town, the December 7, 1926, *New Promoter* reported a city council meeting where homeowners were unhappy that herds of wild horses were running loose in town "destroying lawns, bushes, and other property." A city policeman was appointed to control the horses, and since then, "the numbers of complaints has been greatly diminished [*sic*] . . ."

On June 6, 1928, a report from Winnett, Montana, in sparsely-populated Petroleum County, stated that: "The Statewide campaign to rid Montana ranges of useless wild horses has been successfully carried on in all sections of the state."

Horse abattoirs were set up in eastern Montana. Feral horses were ruining the fragile range at will, and liquidation was considered by many to be the first option. In 1928, a horse abattoir was been established at Manchester, near Great Falls, and another at Broadus around the same time, to handle the major task.

The Ekalaka Eagle

OFFICIAL NEWSPAPER OF CARTER COUNTY

EKALAKA, Carter County, MONTANA, FRIDAY, MAY 23, 1930.

REAL WILD HORSES

Wild horses in the Missouri breaks north of Jordan, are to be rounded up in one big drive to start in June, it is announced by John Marsh, state stock inspector who has just returned from a trip to that country.

The round-up is to be in charge of "Fuzzy" Buffington who is the best known wild horse wrangler in eastern Montana. According to the stock inspector, Buffington is getting his crew of riders ready for the big event when the breaks will be combed from one end to the other in hope of gathering in the herds.

There are places in the breaks where it is almost impossible to penetrate because of false trails, especially in the "hell gate" country. the stock inspector says. He is of the opinion that there are horses there never seen by a human. These horses live and die there.

In previous wild horse round-ups in that territory some wild and vicious horses have been chased but never captured, is the claim.

The whole north side is interested in the approaching round-up and some fine wild prizes are expected this year.

Pertinent article from the May 23, 1930 edition of the Ekalaka Eagle.

Range management began to change with the administration of Franklin Delano Roosevelt. In response to the Dust Bowl conditions, the U.S. Government recognized that previous methods did not work. A new agricultural program, with scientific management as well as market assistance, was an integral part of the New Deal. The aim was to get the moribund sector on its feet again.

Part of the proposed solution was the Taylor Grazing Act, enacted in 1934, "to stabilize the livestock industry dependent upon the public range." This legislation legalized the fencing of public lands and established local grazing districts where ranchers could co-ordinate their use of the grasslands, with a view toward "home rule." Individual ranchers were provided a means to incorporate government land for their own use. In 1946, the General Land Office and Grazing Office merged into the Bureau of Land Management to oversee the effort.

With public lands sensibly fenced, the days of the open range were effectively over. After decades of relentless pursuit, the wild horse herds were greatly diminished. After generations of inbreeding, the range horses were genetically crippled, and many were deformed. The wild horses had become a mere shadow of their former grandeur.

Still, the horses were rounded up for slaughter. On June 9, 1932, the *Reno Evening Gazette* reported a new roundup method was being tested near Lakeview, Oregon, in the Great Basin: the airplane, the effectiveness of which surprised even the cowboys involved on the ground. Roundups, by air and on the ground, legal and otherwise, continued into the 1950s.

Early on, there was interest, from some quarters, in protecting free-roaming horses. On December 5, 1925, *The Havre Daily Promoter* reported that a member of the International Workers of the World, a radical labor organization, set fire to an abattoir in Rockford, Illinois, as a means of protesting the slaughter of wild horses.

A 1938 illustration of gathering wild horses near Winnemucca, Nevada.

In 1950, a descendant of a long-time Nevada ranching family, Velma Bronn Johnston, who became famous as "Wild Horse Annie," witnessed a load of abused wild horses being trucked to slaughter. This ignited an activism to protect wild horses from mistreatment. Beginning at the state level, and continuing to the federal government, she organized a grassroots effort that culminated in 1958 with a federal law which forbade the round-up of wild horses from aircraft.

With increased exposure from the media, along with the nascent environmental movement, the question of what should be done with feral horses running on federal land came into focus. The United States Congress passed the Wild and Free-Roaming Horses and Burros Act, signed into law in 1971. It was supposed to provide a management plan where wild horse herds could be scientifically managed without overgrazing the range, be rendered sterile as necessary, confined and cared for in holding pens, and be adopted by hopeful citizens.

At this point, it may be necessary to clarify the definition of federal land, if possible.

U.S. Government land is managed under several different layers of protection. National parks and monuments, along with other significant sites, are controlled by the National Park Service. A lengthy process is required for improvements, and private business is tightly regulated. National forest lands fall under the auspices of the U.S. Department of Agriculture, which controls the harvest of timber, some development of mines, and some grazing leases.

The majority of range lands in the West are administered by the Bureau of Land Management, which is under the umbrella of the Interior Department (as is the Park Service). The BLM is responsible for leasing permits which can be secured on the basis of the scientific carrying capacity of the lease in question, based on the number of animal-unit/months (AUMs) that can be grazed without depleting the resource—in this case, grass. (One animal-unit=one cow/calf pair.) The better the range, the more animals can be grazed, and vice versa. BLM leases are renewed every ten years, must be part of commensurate property tied to a ranch or farm, and are included as part of an estate. The rancher is responsible for any improvements such as fencing or waterworks. The federal government owns the land, and it is leased for a specific use, whether it be for grazing, timber, or minerals. A separate agency, the National Resources Conservation Service (NRCS), provides the scientific and technical resources to work the land renewably. In other words, the concept of public land is somewhat ambiguous.

The new 1971 law raised as many questions as answers.

The wild horse, or mustang, along with the bald eagle, gray wolf, grizzly bear, and bison, are iconic symbols of the America West, and as such are thought to belong to all Americans. They are, rightfully, regarded with pride as emblems of a strong nation. Native American tribes, especially, feel a kinship with wild horses—after all, they were the first Americans to possess and master them.

But it is also ambiguous to consider the government management of wild horse herds a success.

Wild horses, like any other living creature, require nourishment and have the instinct to reproduce. Left to their own devices, a wild horse herd will double every four years. That puts a lot of stress on the rangeland. By extension, in dry years the fodder may not satisfy the requirements of the wild horses, estimated to number about 40,000 in Nevada alone.

Another aspect is that of the humane treatment of horses. While the outright abuses are somewhat curtailed (even though wild horses are still illegally shot on the range) the question remains of whether it's humane to let wild horses starve for lack of forage.

Some American citizens do not want the horses to be restricted in any way. They believe in the ideal that the horses on public land should be left alone. The unfortunate rancher trying to make a living on the land to which he is entitled would be considered collateral damage.

An additional question concerns the adoptability of the wild horses. Although each has its own disposition, they are all untamed animals, living free all their lives. As a rule, they are hard to acclimate with humans, of whom they are innately afraid. While not unheard of, transforming a wild horse who knows nothing but the open range to a gentle, predictable riding horse is a long shot.

And, last but not least, of what consideration is the rancher, whose family has often occupied the land for over a century, trying to earn a tough living in a hard land?

And so the controversy continues, really, with no end in sight. Whose rights, Native American or non-Native, Westerner, Easterner, or Southerner, Arkansan, Michigander or Mainiac, will prevail? How can land use for ranching, farming, recreation, history, or the environment, fairly benefit both citizens and nature? How can two symbols of the West, the rancher and the mustang, be preserved? Which competing interest will decide?

APPENDIX A.

A SHORT HISTORY OF THE BIRD-HEAD RANCH, or, PROCEDURES AND PERILS OF LIFE IN THE WEST.

In the late 19th century, western North Dakota was a virtually empty province of the northern Great Plains. South of the Missouri River, the landscape was relatively open with some topography and steep hills on the divides. A wide, beautiful band of variegated badlands, several miles across, follows the valley of the Little Missouri River—a crazy maze of pine-covered crags and cliffs. In those days, there wasn't much to attract a farmer.

After the Northern Pacific Railroad was built through there in 1879, a few determined and well-capitalized ranchers began filtering into the badlands. The new railroad furnished transportation, and the Little Missouri River was a source of good water and shelter in the winter. The dozen or so pioneer ranches (two owned by Theodore Roosevelt) were located on the river at the high-water mark. The area between the Missouri and the Little Missouri was unoccupied.

The first ranch in the open plains was the Reynolds Brothers' Long X, at the site of the terminus of a branch of the fabled Texas Trail. It was located on a wide flat southwest of present-day Watford City, North Dakota—a wonderful grassland. For close to seven years, they had the place to themselves.

Along the Missouri River itself, the European influence was somewhat earlier. A major thorough-fare since time immemorial, Lewis and Clark are credited with its first scientific exploration. Once it had been proven to be possible, fur trappers began their exploitation and numerous temporary trading posts were established to service the trade. At the strategic confluence of the Missouri and Yellowstone Rivers, the American Fur Company established Fort Union in 1829, just ahead of the steamboat. The

Long X entry into the 1892 North Dakota Stockgrowers' Association Brand Book.

228

State of North Dakota,
} ss.
County of ....

Know All Men by These Presents, That we the Morning Star Cattle Co a resident of *Roberts* ...., County of *St. Croix* .... State of *Wisconsin* ...., do ...... hereby adopt the following Mark and Brand, for the purpose of marking and branding Live Stock, to-wit:

DESCRIPTION.	FAC-SIMILE.	MARK.	WHERE AND HOW USED.
Birds Head			On both sides or either of cattle. Left thigh horses.

And we ...... hereby claim the exclusive right to use said Marks and Brands within this State. Said live stock range in *Wallace County North Dakota*

County of *Wallace* .... State of North Dakota.
Witness our hand at *Bismarck* .... in said County, this 11th day of *May* .... 1893.

IN PRESENCE OF
W. L. De Puy

Morning Star Cattle Co
by J. S. Gurn

Filed for record this 11th day of *May* 1893, and certified copy of original transmitted to Register of Deeds of the Court ...... of ......

Morning Star brand registration with the State of North Dakota, 1893.

Fort Union trade was simple: whiskey, iron goods, cloth, and trinkets upriver, and an untold fortune in furs back down. Wood yards every few miles fed the steamboat boilers. Around the time of the Civil War, the U.S. army established a presence to contain the restive prairie tribes. Finally, the local tribes, the Mandans, Hidatsas, and Arikaras, were confined to the Fort Berthold reserve in 1870. The Northern Railroad was built along the newly-uncontested Yellowstone River in 1881 and 1882. What would become the Great Northern was built north of the Missouri River in 1887, facilitating settlement in the still-isolated region.

A few early ranchers decided to take the risk of establishing ranches on the untamed prairies adjacent to the wide Missouri. One of the earliest was McEwen Uhlman, a native Nova Scotian born in 1854. He, his wife Millie, and their young family emigrated to Wisconsin in 1884. A few years later, leaving his loved ones behind, Uhlman, as part of the newly organized Morning Star Cattle Company, in 1891 used federal land scrip to acquire a likely spot on the Missouri River from the Stroud Brothers, veterans of the Long X cattle drives. The ranch registered its distinctive "bird-head" brand with the state of North Dakota in 1893. A line-camp was built at Ragged Butte Spring at the site of present-day Alexander, North Dakota, in about 1895. Their herds were grazed on unfenced free government grass, along with those of the Long X and a few other outfits.

The Bird-Head was, by all accounts, a fairly typical successful ranching operation in the 1890s. Mac Uhlman is remembered having a no-nonsense, curious nature, somewhat dour in the vein of business tycoons, and not noted for his sense of humor.

Early-day ranching followed the cycle of nature, a routine that is still used today.

After the spring thaw, generally in early April, calving season got underway. Cows had to be watched closely when giving birth. Complications demanded immediate attention, and it was vitally important that the newborn calves be kept dry. After a normal birth, calves would be on their feet within an hour, chasing their mothers. This process could take place over the space of several weeks. Mother and child would be free to roam at will in search of nourishment.

Around the end of May, the spring roundup began. The local stockgrowers association would assign roundup districts, usually following principal drainage basins. Cowboys from member ranches would start on the divides and gather cattle as they worked their way downhill. Generally, near the mouth of the creek, cattle were driven into the roundup corrals. At this point branding began. Calves stayed close to their branded mothers, and in this way were identified as owned by one ranch or other. The calves were cut out one by one by expert horsemen; another would keep the mother at bay. A fire was nearby with the respective irons being kept red hot. The calf was roped and dragged to the fire, and the brand was applied in accordance with the registration. Each ranch had a representative, or "rep," which prevented mistakes of ownership. At this time the bull calves were turned into steers. The hot, noisy, traumatic procedure then being complete, the newly branded calf rejoined its mother and set out to pasture.

Summer work for cowhands was a steady routine. The ranch was astir long before dawn ("Morning Star Cattle Company—first star in the morning!"). A youngster would get on a gentle "jingle" horse to gather the "ponies" needed for the day's tasks. After a generous, tasty breakfast prepared by the camp cook, the cowboys saddled up and went to work following cattle over the prairies and ensuring their safety. Sick cows, generally noted by their behavior, were brought to the ranch for doctoring. Range cattle could get into all sorts of trouble falling into ravines, getting mired in mud holes, tangling with wild animals, being lost in the badlands. After dinner, the cowboys would fall into a deep sleep; it had been a hard day. All for about $30 a month (not really a bad wage for the time).

Other ranch hands had to cultivate hay for the winter feed base, easily the lowest-status job at the place. Most proud cowboys were chagrined at the prospect of following a mule. But it was an important task, as ranchers remembered all too well the lessons of the hard winter of 1887.

After a summer tending cattle and watching them gain weight, the fall roundup took place. Calves were separated from their mothers to be weaned. This task, unexpected and unwelcome by the youngsters, was necessary for their maturation. Besides, their mothers were likely pregnant again and were beginning to turn the "young-uns" away.

Older cattle were then being readied for market, off to the stockyards of the Midwest.

The ranchers along the Missouri River would order a stock train from the Great Northern Railroad (a cattle train would typically carry up to 800 head—twenty per car). Cows would be kept off water for three days to overcome their fear of what was to come. At the appointed time, the cows would be "gathered at the river." This colorful operation had to be performed with precision. (It has been described as "more than colorful—it was dangerous, damned dangerous.") Mounted cowboys would ease the cattle toward the river, trying to keep control of the situation. The thirsty cows would rush into the water and would have to be driven forward. Some would get to milling and it was up to the cowhands to keep them pointed the right way. Other riders had to be downstream to keep cattle from drifting with the current. When they got to the other side of the river (the Missouri River no less!), the stock would be slowly

Views from the Bird-Head Ranch area from the early 1900s.

trailed to the loading chutes at the station at Avoca, North Dakota, several miles east of Williston. There the ranch owner and several cowboys would ride the caboose to the destination. (The term "cow-poke" originated from these cowboys poking a long rod through the slats of the cattle car to keep them on their feet.) After arriving at St. Paul or Chicago, the rancher counted his proceeds and his help would go off to enjoy the city, often blowing their entire paychecks. After the long ride home, the slack season began. The cowboys were laid off, and were free to find odd work with neighboring ranches, or to head south to their Texas homes, escaping the winter entirely. Wherever they were, they awaited the warmer weather and for the cycle to begin anew.

While ranching was a potentially lucrative pursuit, the day-to-day operations were fraught with peril. First and foremost was the capricious Northern Plains climate. Winters could be extreme: temperatures could drop to forty below zero and lower. Cowhands had to make sure of the well-being of the winter herds, making sure they were fed (from a hay wagon) and watered by chopping through a water hole with an axe. There would always be the chance for cattle to find their way onto the frozen rivers, only to be extricated from snow-covered air holes. Prairie blizzards could seemingly come out of nowhere, with blinding snow and plummeting temperatures. It was quite often "not fit for man nor beast."

Summer, too, was rife with hazards. A hot, still day could be foreboding. Violent thunderstorms would lash the countryside without warning. A man on horseback was a perfect target for a lightning bolt on the treeless plains, which were often reported in the local newspapers: on July 12, 1893, the Fort Benton *River Press* reported that two cowboys on the Milk River roundup were struck by lightning near the Little Rocky Mountains (they both survived but one of their horses was killed). Hail could knock the hell out of cowboys and their livestock—another frequent occurrence. Pouring rains would turn the entire prairie into a gooey morass, necessitating the rescue of cows in trouble. Another instance of the partnership between horse and rider.

Prairie fires were another dreaded hazard. A lightning strike from beyond the horizon, pushed by a strong wind, could consume 150,000 acres overnight, threating life and property. In order to put one out, a wet hide was pulled along the fire's edge, but it was mostly too little too late. A bad fire would

THE RIVER PRESS.

Vol. XIII.   Fort Benton, Montana, Wednesday, July 12, 1893.   No. 38.

On June 27th, the day before the Milk river round-up disbanded, some of the riders were holding a bunch of cattle at a point just south of the Little Rockies, and at the same time a thunder storm was prevailing. During the storm a flash of lightning knocked two of the cowboys from their horses. The riders were not very seriously injured, and both will recover, but one of the horses which they were riding was killed.

Local item from July 12, 1893.

THE RIVER PRESS.

Vol. XIV.　　　Fort Benton, Montana, Wednesday, August 29, 1894.　　　No. 45.

A RUINED RANGE.

Disastrous Prairie Fires Destroy Many Miles of Grass.

The Marias range is literally destroyed between the Teton and Marias rivers, and from the narrow guage railroad eastward to the confluence of the two streams. There have been some disastrous prairie fires in Montana in the past, but never before was there, at any one time, so much range destroyed. Besides the portion referred, to, extensive fires have occurred within the past two weeks, south of the Teton and north of Marias, but the scope of range destroyed, as noted above, is the largest in extent ever known here.

On Tuesday morning it was thought that the fire had been subdued, but in the afternoon it was learned that it was still advancing eastward, and Capt. James Townsend gathered a crew of fifteen of the Marias riders and started for the fire. They struck the fire a few miles across the Teton and worked faithfully until nearly five o'clock this morning, when they at last got the flames subdued. The extremely dry weather made their task a fearfully hard one.

Wednesday forenoon the boys returned, and gave it as their opinion that the fire originated from the narrow guage railroad, and that the territory burnt over is 40 miles in length, by from 15 to 20 miles in width. Usually the number of cattle on the range between the two rivers is about 7,000 or 8,000 head, so the amount of loss to stockmen can be calculated when it is seen that these cattle must feed on other range, already crowded.

All day Tuesday the northwest wind from the blazing prairie blew directly down onto Fort Benton, and was hot almost to suffocation. Today the air is dense with smoke, and this afternoon information was received that the fire had again broken out, at Sheep coulee some fifteen miles northeast of Fort Benton. At this writing a crew is starting from this point to fight the fire. The impression among cattle men is that unless rains soon prevail the Marias range, for this year, is doomed to destruction.

Description of 1894 prairie fire in northern Montana.

require a rancher to move his herds to a new range, if one were to be found. "Incendiaries" (range arsonists) were dealt with summarily—the September 30, 1882, issue of the Miles City *Yellowstone Journal* reported that one J.J. Bowles was lynched in the Judith Basin: "It appears that Bowles had set the prairie on fire [intentionally or not is not stated]. . ."

Routine injuries among ranch hands were frequent, and professional care was usually far away. It was not rare to see former cowboys hobbling around town, their careers cut short by a poorly-set broken arm or leg. Kicks from cattle or horses would cause internal injuries that would doom them to a lifetime of misery. Accidents could be fatal. A July 4, 1891, item in the Miles City *Live Stock Reporter* related that Charles Rutledge, "one of the top hands of the LU ranch . . . was assigned the duty of cutting out the stray cattle, and was chasing one, when [his horse] fell. His horse was on a dead jump, and fell over the steer, rolling on Charley." Rattlesnake bites were also common—in July 1892 the *Yellowstone Journal* mentioned that Johnnie Gavin, otherwise known as "K Bar Johnnie" was bitten by a "venomous rattlesnake." He rode to Blatchford, and was carried to Glendive by train for "medical assistance": ". . . although any fatal results were obviated, he still has a hard looking arm."

Predators abounded. A pack of wolves could decimate a calf herd—bounties were posted for wolf hides. Coyotes also like small game, mostly rodents, but a small calf or lamb would do just as well. Grizzly bears, native to the prairie, roamed at will, looking for berries, their preferred delicacy, but, finding none, would just as soon have a tasty beef or horse dinner, or a human if one became available. (Wolves and grizzly bears were hunted to extinction by the 1920s. In the 1980s environmentalists sought to bring back the grey wolf to its native habitat. Faced with strident opposition from ranchers, wolves were reintroduced. The controversy is far from settled: protections are being rolled back, and western lawmakers are re-establishing hunting seasons for historic predators.)

And last but not least, ranchers suffered from depredations from horse- and cattle thieves. These were dealt with harshly. In 1901, the Bird-Head outfit was plagued by a gang of thieves and rustlers, the result of which was related above.

In spite of all the tough winters, bad weather, fires, predators, personal injuries, and range thievery, the Bird Head prospered under Mac Uhlman. Throughout the 1890s, the Bird Head shipped many thousands of cattle on the Great Northern. He and his neighbors, the old Long X outfit, Stroud Brothers, and Jay Grantier (another former Long X cowboy, who claimed his pre-emption in 1890), pretty much had the place to themselves. They were free to pursue their accustomed livelihoods as the frontier began to dissolve around them.

Around 1900, a few new ranchers began to filter onto the prairie. The newcomers, still generally stockmen, put up fences to protect their hay meadows. In doing so, the pioneers found it harder to graze their herds over the grasslands.

In 1898, the Long X sold its Cherry Creek operation to the Converse Cattle Company, an old-time New England cattle syndicate. Shortly thereafter, they left the North Dakota range entirely, moving their operation to the Missouri Breaks, south of Malta, Montana, in 1901.

In 1901, the United States government issued the first survey for the North Dakota area south of the Missouri River, allowing formal filing for homesteads. Immediately, home-seekers poured into the area, intent on farming, not ranching. The arid, rocky sod was broken by the iron plow, and the race to heartbreak was on.

Barbed-wire fences were strung along the 160-acre homestead borders. The free-ranging cattle were impeded from grazing. The pioneers, now being crowded out, shook their collective heads at the unfolding spectacle. Their domain was shrinking. A new generation was about to make its own mistakes.

In 1904, Mac Uhlman sold his interest in the Morning Star Cattle Company, and moved his operation near the 1890s-era Shafer Ranch, to a site about eight miles east of present-day Watford City, North Dakota. He remained there only long enough to build a sprawling log home, and soon after, purchased land from Jay Grantier adjacent to the old Bird-Head Ranch. At the same time, he bought land near isolated Dimmick Lake, farther east from Shafer's, for grazing land, possibly at the site of a Bird-Head line camp from the early days.

Signs of settlement began appearing on the prairie. There were scattered schools for the children, isolated country churches were opening, a ferry was in operation at Williston, and new counties were being organized from the vast old ones. At last, in 1907 Mac Uhlman brought his family from Wisconsin.

Long a lover of fine horses, and always looking for an opportunity, in 1908 Mac entered the thoroughbred horse business, with a view of racing at the county fairs and festivals now taking place throughout the countryside. Eager to "get in on the ground floor," he took the train to Kentucky, where he purchased a thoroughbred stallion and four mares.

Over the next couple years, he seems to have done well in his new venture. In the fall of 1911, he and Art Bond, his ranch foreman, travelled to Europe to improve his stock. As it turned out, it was a trip of a lifetime. Along the way, he and his small retinue enjoyed the sights of Europe, and experienced a ride in an aeroplane (wearing a formal suit). Making stops in Belgium and France, he bought the equivalent of a (train) car load of fine horses, and, accompanied by a French trainer, took the liner for the long voyage home.

They made it as far as western Pennsylvania, where, on December 6, 1911, the train on which they were riding plowed into a minor wreck ahead. The crushing impact claimed the lives of six: the entire Uhlman party and three railroad employees, along with seventeen of the prized horses.

The family's (and the community's) grief was deep and sincere—Mac was truly a man not only of his times, but one of the future. He left the ranch in able hands. Millie was an astute manager, and the young ones had come of age. Today, the ranch remains in their family, passed down through many heirs, still a home on the North Dakota prairie.

There have been profound changes to western North Dakota since the days of the Bird-Head and Long X—after all, it's been over a century.

In 1913, the "Wild Cow" railroad, technically a branch of the Great Northern, was built to the new village of Watford City to carry farm products to the main line at Snowden, Montana. (Two massive bridges from this project, over the Missouri and Yellowstone Rivers, remain today.) The "Dirty Thirties" of the Great Depression were terrible times on the Northern Plains, where many people lived on the edge of starvation until the massive New Deal Fort Peck Dam project provided some economic relief. But by that time most of the homesteaders had abandoned the farms they had toiled on for so long to maintain. In the 1950s, another flood control dam was built by the Corps of Engineers at Garrison, North Dakota, inundating the Missouri River agricultural land used by Mandan, Hidatsa, and Arikara (now known as the Three Affiliated Tribes) for centuries. Now they live in new settlements high and dry on the wind-swept prairie.

In the early 1950s, petroleum was discovered in the area, turning the region upside down. Over a series of booms and busts, and using ever-advancing technology, the oil industry has brought the open range full-circle into the post-industrial age, with lots of economic benefits and massive social disruption.

In June of 2019, a good friend, an aging cowboy who was raised near Alexander, and I took a trip into the "Bakken," named for the geologic formation from where the oil is being pumped (along with vast amounts of natural gas and waste brine). The idea was to view the sites where history took place long ago, and besides, although being a long-term resident of Glendive, I had never been to Watford City. For fifty miles or so north of Beach, North Dakota, the land seemed pretty much as it had always been—wide-open treeless prairie. Then, abruptly, we ran into the "oil patch," and its presence was everywhere: historic old ranches surrounded by oil rigs serviced by big trucks that raised clouds of dust visible for miles. Natural gas flares proliferated to get rid of the unwanted by-product. We were able to get close, but not too close, to one—it was roaring, hissing, and hot.

The trip took an emotional turn when we got to Alexander. The Ragged Butte Spring, which had blessed the arid land with good water for ages, was now capped. My friend turned away in disgust. Venturing on to Watford City, we found an old farm settlement that had been transformed into a brand new town of fast-food joints and strip malls, a gleaming new hospital that treats all sorts of oilfield injuries, big motels that evoke the names of pioneers long ago (among whom was a president of the United States), along with massive equipment depots, pipe yards, and oil patch miscellany. Not much remains to remind one of the old days. After a little research at the modern courthouse, we turned for home. Along the way, we checked out the site of the old Long X ranch, and were treated to a prairie thunderstorm. All in all it was a somewhat bittersweet journey. We were provided a lesson about the true meaning, and cost, of progress: I suppose it depends on who you ask.

APPENDIX B.

FRONTIER NEWSPAPERS.

Much of the historical material presented here originated in pioneer newspapers. As a source of pertinent information, they really have little parallel.

Since the dawn of the American frontier, whether it be the Appalachian woods, cypress swamps, rolling farmlands, open prairie, or gold rush boom towns, settlement has followed a fairly predictable path. First, frontiersmen looked for possible ways to earn a livelihood. Most of them explored along rivers and streams which were easiest to get to (and away from). They were seeking resources, including farmland, timber, and possible minerals. Others with the same idea soon followed. These pioneers generally picked the best places to settle, and quickly drew together for colonization schemes and mutual defense—the emergent government, either federal, state, or territorial, was only too happy to provide land grants, and besides, the common notion was that the Native tribes were not using the land for anything, anyway.

Within a short time, depending on the availability of resources and how much work it took to exploit them, a few settlements sprang up. These were generally rustic and almost totally utilitarian with an eye for basic survival. Generally a saloon was the first business establishment, followed quickly by a small general store, blacksmith shop, livery stable, and more saloons (churches and schools came a little later). A local transportation network (primarily stage coach lines) was also quick in coming—before long, these merged into a regional network that connected with the wider world.

At about this point, a newcomer would likely arrive with a flat-plate printing press suitable for producing a newspaper. The response from the early settlers was generally receptive.

The lifeblood of any nascent community is a sense of importance, and nothing provided it better than a local newspaper. In general, these were low-budget, printed weekly on fools-cap paper (about the lowest quality available), but they served a vital purpose. Items of local interest were typeset by hand, using countless fonts (which gave the papers a decidedly primitive look). Type was placed in the press, piece by piece, an endless process. Linotype was invented in 1886, which speeded things up a bit. (The used lead type was melted and recycled—a toxic procedure, no doubt.) Pre-formed symbols, also inserted in the press, were commonly used in papers of that era: an arm and hammer for a blacksmith, a horse and buggy denoted a livery, a crucible for a druggist, horses and cattle figures for brand advertisements, along with fraternal symbols, railroad insignia, and many others (southern newspapers depicted a man carrying a bindle for notifications of runaway slaves). Entire "boilerplate" pages were brought by wagon, railroad, or steamboat, and duly placed on the press. Early newspapers contained few illustrations—reproduction of photographs was impossible much before 1900—but steel engravings were sometimes used instead.

The typical frontier newspaper had four pages: a single large broadsheet folded over (a prospering metropolis like Fort Benton or Miles City might use *two* broadsheets with eight pages). The front page may consist of boilerplate news or educational articles. The second page typically carried regional or national editorials, a list of local office holders, and maybe local advertisements. Page three contained significant news, local items of varying importance, personal ads, town gossip, more local advertisements, and possibly railroad or stage schedules. The back page had more boilerplate articles or serials along with national advertisements (many for cheap patent medicines or get-rich-quick schemes). Advertisements reflected the local commerce and culture. In the west, many papers printed subscribed brand notices ("cuts") to help ranchers recover lost or stolen stock. In general, a predictable, neat affair, was anxiously awaited every week.

Range cowboys especially sought newspapers. Not often getting to town, their off-hours were spent in a bunkhouse or maybe under stars. Recreation was limited and included playing cards, drinking (often on the sly), mending clothes, reading, singing or playing the guitar, sleeping, or fighting. Newspapers were considered a fine source of mental enrichment. They were passed from hand to hand until they fell apart.

The editorial content of the newspapers mirrored those of the community—in other words, generally conservative. Western editors, thoroughly imbued with the doctrine of "Manifest Destiny," railed against tribal depredations and the need to confine the Natives to distant reservations. Additionally, the newspapers were tireless advocates of the ranching industry, railroad building, the need for law and order, statehood support, and shameless civic promotion.

Some newspapers were unabashedly organs for political parties. A masthead that read "Republican," "Democrat," or "Populist" left no doubt of their party affiliation. These papers were the voice of the party, vociferously supporting their candidates and denigrating their opponents, often resorting to personal slander. It was not unheard of for newspaper editors to be beaten, or even assassinated, for expressing their views.

News articles in frontier papers are endlessly fascinating. History occurs constantly, and newspapers reported it through a local lens, unfiltered by time. They carried all types of news: cowboy anecdotes, "railroad rumblings," local tragedies, criminal activity, personal items, town gossip, and possibly lame jokes. Larger newspapers, such as the *Bismarck Tribune* or *Great Falls Tribune* (a common moniker) were likely connected to a national wire service such as the Associated Press.

Public notices were a major part of a newspaper's revenue. Many of these were homestead claims with a rancher's exact location and his time of arrival. These, along with the brand advertisements, are useful in reconstructing a pattern of settlement for a given geographical area.

The quality of the early newspapers varied widely. Most had a somewhat professional appearance and were well written, with maybe an eye toward posterity. Others were strictly low-budget sheets that didn't contain much of anything useful—little news and lots of party screed. Over time, many of these small papers merged with their competitors, resulting in masthead that read *Globe-Republican*, from Dodge City, Kansas, or the *Banner-Democrat* (Lake Providence, La.).

Local newspapers are an essential tool for researchers. No matter what the event, famous or obscure, it found its way into a newspaper somewhere. Widely known historical events, such as Civil War military campaigns (many contemporary papers carried soldier's letters) or the Little Big Horn Battle, were quickly reported—news of national importance presented from a local perspective.

A problem with old newspapers is preservation. Some newspaper offices carry bound volumes of their early editions. Local museums might have them too. Many newspapers were preserved on microfilm—very valuable, but viewing them can be a cumbersome, time-consuming process, and besides, functional microfilm readers are becoming harder to find.

But digitization has revolutionized historical research. There are many internet sites that contain digitized original papers—the Library of Congress' "Chronicling America" has over 3,800 of titles dating as far back as the 1700s. Many states sponsor free sites as well. Genealogy research sites often carry a large assortment of titles, but most charge a subscription fee. For a researcher, the cost is generally worth it.

Still, original newspapers are fragile. Most were thrown away or have decayed over time. Some titles, such as the 1895 Landusky *Miner and Prospector,* which circulated in a lawless mining camp in Montana, or the 1893 *Tallulah (La.) Blade,* a turbulent time in the south, have been lost to antiquity, the only evidence of their existence being excerpts from other nearby papers.

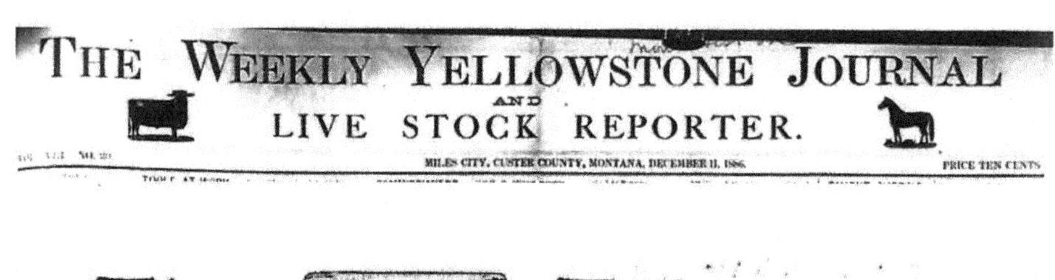

Elegant Mastheads from early Montana newspapers.

SOURCES OF INFORMATION

Chapter 1

Curtis, Helena. *Biology*. Worth Publishing, New York: 1979.

Dott, Robert H., and Batten, Roger L. *Evolution of the Earth*. McGraw-Hill, New York: 1981.

Grassland. https://en.wikipedia.ord/wiki/Grassland

Evolution of the Horse. https://en.wikipedia.org/wiki/Evolution_of_the_horse. Also, https://en.wikipedia.org/wiki/Paleocene

Equidae. https://en.wikipwdi.org/wiki/Equidae

"Horse Family tree." www.harunyaha.com/image/confessions_of_evolutionists/...

The Evolution of Horses. http://www.amnh.org/exhibitionx/horse/the-evolution-of- horses

The evolution of the horse, with particular emphasis on the changing foot structure. http://2.bp.blogspot.com/-fcAo6s6Ben8/VE49THzCUDI...

Hyracotherium. https://en.wikipedia.org/wiki/Hyracotheruim

Mesohippus. https://en.wikipedia.org/wikw/Mesohippus

Dinohippus. https://en.wikpedia.org/wiki/Dinohippus

Domestication of the Horse. https://en.wikipedia.org/wiki/Domestication-of-the-Horse z

Tracing the History of the Horse Evolution and Domestication: The Year in Review, 2012, www.britannica.com

Wadsworth (Nev.) *Dispatch*, August 18, 1897. www.chroniclingamerica.loc.gov/

Chapter 2

The Second Voyage of Columbus. www.indepthinfo.com/columbuschristopher/second-voyage.htm

Hispanola. https://en.wikipedia.org/wiki/Hispanola

Hispanola: The First Colony. http://www.latinamericanstudies.org/first_colony.htm

Santo Domingo. https://wikipedia.org.wiki/Santo-Domingo

History of Cuba. https://en.wikipedia.org/wiki/History_of_Cuba

Diego Valázquez de Cuellar. http://en.wikipedia.org/wiki/Diego_Vel%C3%Alzquez-de_Cu%C3%A911ar

Juan Ponce de León. https://wikipedia.org/wiki/Juan_Ponce_de_Leon

Hernan Cortés. https://en.wikipedia.org/wiki/Hern%C3%A1n_Cort%C3%A9s

Horses of the Conquistadors. http://spanishvisionfarm.com/Atricles/History/conquistadors.html

Pánfilo de Narváez. https://en.wikipedia.org/wiki/Pánfilo_de_Narváez

Reséndez, Andrés. *A Land So Strange: The Epic Journey of Cabeza de Vaca*. Basic Books. New York: 2007.

Álvar Núñez Cabeza de Vaca. https://en.wikipedia.org/wiki/%C3%811var_N%C3%BA%C3%B1ez_Cabeza_de_Vaca

Cabeza de Vaca's route map of his return to Mexico. http://www.texasbeyondhistory.net/cabeza-cooking/images/krieger-map.jpg

Hernando de Soto. http://en.wikipedia.org/wiki/Hernando_de_Soto

The Expedition of Hernando de Soto to Southwestern North America, 1538-43. http://www.sjsu.edu/faculty/watkins.desoto.htm

Map of the Hernando De Soto Expedition, 1539-1543. http://ocala.com/assets/images/widgets?Ocala/Maps/CompleteDeSotoMap.jpg.

The Final Report of the Official Commission. [De Soto Route-1936]. http://floridahistory.com/inset99.html

Encyclopedia of Arkansas History and Culture. *Route of the De Soto Expedition*. https://encyclopediaofarkansas.net/entries/route-of-the-desoto-expedition-7679/

Hernando de Soto. NNDB- Tracking the entire world. https://www.nndb.com/people/528/000109201/

The Amarillo Globe. "Site of Massacre is Believed Found." April 19, 1935.

The Mysterious Journey of Friar Marcos de Niza. Planetary Science Institute. https://psi.edu/about/staff/hartmann/ Coronado/journeyof marcodeniza.html

Francisco Vázquez de Coronado. https://en.wikipedia,org.wiki/Francisco_V%C3%A1zquez_de_Coronado

Seven Cities of Gold (myth). https://en.wikipedia.org/wiki/Seven_Cities_of_Gold_(myth)

Zuni-Cibola Complex. https://en.wikipedia.org/wiki/Zuni-Cibola_Complex

Quivera. https://eb/wikipedia.org/wiki/Quivera

Conquistador. https://en.wikipedia.org.wiki/Conquistador#Firearms

Chamuscado and Rodriguez Expedition. https://en.wikipedia.org/wiki/Chamuscado_and_Rodr%C3%ASguez _Expedition

Umana and Leyva expedition. https://en.wikipedia.org/wiki/Humana_and _Leyva_Expedition

History of New Mexico. https://wikipedia.en.org/wiki/History_of_New_Mexico

Juan de Oñate. http://wikipedia.org/wiki/Juan_de_O%C3%B1ate

Juan de Oñate. http://www.elizathetan-era.org.uk/juan-de-onate.htm

Encomienda. https://en.wikipedia.org/wiki/Encomienda

Puebloans. https://en.wikipedia.org/wiki/Puebloans

https://legendsofamerica.com/na-puebloindians/

Pueblo Indians – Oldest Culture in the U.S.

Pueblo Revolt. https://en.wikipedia.org/wiki/Pueblo_Revolt

The Tropical Sun, Juno (on Lake Worth), Florida, May 26, 1892. https://ufdc.ufl.edu/UF00075915/00485?search= tropicalsun+=sun

Chapter 3

Bradley, James H. "James F. Bradley Manuscript Book 'F,'" pp. 197-250. *Contributions to the Historical Society of Montana*, Vol. 8. Helena: State Publishing Company, 1917.

Bradley, James H. "Indian Traditions" in James H. Bradley Manuscript, pp. 288-299. *Contributions to the Historical Society of Montana*, Vol. 9. Helena: State Publishing Company, 1923.

Catlin, George. *North American Indians, being letters and notes on their manners, customs, and conditions, written during eight years' travels amongst the wildest tribes of Indians of North America, 1932-1839.* London: Chatto and Windus, 1876; Philadelphia: Leary, Stuart & Co. (publisher) and Edinburgh: Oliver and Boyd (lithography), 1913.

Denig, Edwin T. (John C. Ewers, editor). "Of the Crow Nation" in *Five Indian Tribes of the Upper Missouri: Sioux, Arikaras, Assiniboines, Crees, Crows*, pp. 137-204. Norman: University of Oklahoma Press, 1961.

Densmore, Francis. "Teton Sioux Music." *Smithsonian Institution, Bulletin of American Ethnology, Bulletin 61.* Washington: U.S. Government Printing Office, 1918. (Quote in Velie 1991: 84)

Ewers, John C. *The Horse in Blackfeet Indian Culture: With Comprehensive Material from other Western Tribes.* Washington: Government Printing Office, 1955; Norman: University of Oklahoma Press.

Ewers, John C. *The Blackfeet: Raiders on the Northwestern Plains.* University of Oklahoma Press. Norman, Okla.: 1958.

Heidenreich, C. Adrian. *Smoke Signals in Crow (Apsáalooke) Country: Beyond the Capture of Horses from the Lewis and Expedition.* Billings, Montana, published by the Author, 2006.

Heidenreich, C. Adrian. "The Western Tipi Pole of Crow Territory: Tribes, Fur Trade, and the Three Forks Area; Including Three Maps and Annotations for Tribal Encampments and Encounters." *Selected Papers of the 2010 Fur Trade Symposium at the Three Forks* (Jim Hardee, Editor.) Three Forks, Montana: Three Forks Area Historical Society, 2011.

Heidenreich, Adrian C., and Bugenstein, Michael D. *Map of the Historical Crow Nation and its Connection to the Great North-West* (including sources). Artcraft Printers, Billings, Mont: 2005.

Irving, Washington, (Richard Dilworth Rust, Editor). *Astoria, or Anecdotes of an American Enterprise beyond the Rocky Mountains.* Lincoln, University of Nebraska Press, 1982.

Jackson, John C. *The Piikani Blackfeet: A Culture Under Siege.* Mountain Press Publishing Co. Missoula, Mont.: 2000.

Lawrence, Elizabeth Atwood. "The Horse in Crow Indian Culture, Past and Present." *Hoofbeats and Society: Studies of Human-Horse Interactions* pp. 1-56. Bloomington: Indiana University Press, 1985.

McGinnis, Anthony R. *Counting Coup and Cutting Horses, Intertribal Warfare on the Northern Plains.* University of Nebraska Press, Lincoln and London: 1990.

McIntosh, John. *Origin of the North American Indians.* Nafish and Cornish, New York, 1856.

Moulton, Gary (Editor). *The Journals of the Lewis and Clark Expedition, Vol. 7.* Lincoln: University of Nebraska Press, 1991.

Nabokov, Peter (Editor, after William Wildschut). *Two Leggings: the Making of a Crow Warrior.* New York: Thomas Y. Crowell, 1967.

Parkman, Francis. *LaSalle and the Discovery of the Great West.* New York: The Modern Library, 1985. (Originally published 1879.)

Roe, Frank Albert. *The Indian and the Horse.* University of Oklahoma Press, Norman, Okla.: 1955.

Colonial Horses in the New World- Part 1. http://mikekearbystexas.blogspot.com/2011/065/colonial-horses-in-the-new-world-part-1. html

Mustang. https://en/wikipedia.org/wiki/Mustang: Return to the New World. http://www2.powayusd.com/teachers/bsnatibanez/Reintroduction%20of%20Horse.htm

The Spanish Colonial Horse and the Plains Indian Culture. www.paulrittman.com/IndianCultureandtheHorse.pdf

Map of the Dispersion of the Horse. http://thefurtrapper.com/wp-content/2015/11/Horse-Map.jpg

American Indian Horse: History 1620-1800, the Indian Horse Period. http://www.redoaktree.org/indianhorse/history 2.htm.

Amcrican Indian Horse: History 1800-1890, the Indian Horse Period. http://www.redoaktree.org/indianhorse/history3.htm.

American Indian Horse. History 1890-Present. http://www.redoaktree.org/indianhorse/history4.htm

APACHE INDIANS. The handbook of Texas online. Texas State Historical Association. https://tshaonline.org/handbook/online/articles/bma33

Apache. https://en.wikipedia.org.wiki/Apache

Native American Legends: Apache- the Fiercest Warriors in the Southwest. http://www.legendsofamerica.com/na-apache.html

Comanche. https://en.wikipedia.org/wiki/Comanche

Comanche history. https://en.wikipedia.org/wiki/Comanche_history

The Comanche – Horsemen of the Plains. http://www.legendsofamerica.com/na-comanche.html

Ouachita Tribe. https://www.accessgenalogy.com/native/ouachita-tribe.htm

Wichita Tribe. https://www.accessgenalogy.com/native/wichita-tribe.htm

Pawnee Tribe. https://accessgenalogy.com/native/pawnee-tribe.htm

Pawnee. http://www.newworldencyclopedia.org/entry/Pawnee

Arapahoe. https://en.wikipedia.org/wiki/Arapaho

Gros Ventre. https://en.wikipedia.org/wiki/Gros_Ventre

Benton Record. Fort Benton, Montana, various issues, 1875-1884. www.newspapers.com

River Press. Fort Benton, Montana, various issues, 1880-1886. www.newspapers.com

The Daily Gazette. Billings, M.T., Aug. 14, Nov. 6, 1885; Sept. 11, 29, 1886. www.newspapers.com

Catlin, George. Ba-da-ah-chon-du (He Who Outjumps All), a Crow Chief on Horseback. https://www.george catlin.org.

Miller, Alfred Jacob. "Snake Indian Pursuing a Crow Horse Thief." https://alfred jacobmiller.com/artworks/ snake-indian-pursuing-a-crow-horse-thief-2/

Chapter 4

Abbott, E.C. ("Teddy Blue") and Smith, Helena Huntington. *We Pointed The North: Reflections of a Cowpuncher.* University of Oklahoma Press, Norman and London: 1939.

Burlingame, Merrill G. *The Montana Frontier.* State Publishing Co. Helena: 1942. Coburn, Walt. *Pioneer Cattleman in Montana: The Story of the Circle C Ranch.* University of Oklahoma Press, Norman: 1968.

Cheney, Roberta Carkeek. *Names on the Face of Montana.* Mountain Press Publishing Co. Missoula: 1983.

Dimsdale, Prof. Thomas J. *The Vigilantes of Montana.* Original date: 1869.

Linderman, Frank B. *Plenty Coups, Chief of the Crows.* New York: John Day, 1930. Nabokov, *Two Leggings.*

Sharp, Paul F. *Whoop-Up Country.* University of Oklahoma Press, Norman: 1955. Stuart, Granville. *Forty Years on the Frontier.* Edited by Paul C. Phillips. Arthur H Clark Co. Cleveland: 1925.

Benton Weekly Record, Fort Benton, Montana, 1875-84.Various issues.www.newspapers.com

River Press, Fort Benton, Montana. Various Issues 1880-88. www.newspapers.com, also in original volumes 1888-1896.

The Daily Tribune, Great Falls, Mont. Nov. 20, 1892. www.newspapers.com

History of Rocky Boys Indian Reservation. Chippewa-Cree Cultural Resources Preservation Department. www. neiyahw.com/historical.html

Chapter 5

Abbott and Smith. *We Pointed Them North, op. cit.*

Hegne, Barbara. *Border Outlaws of Montana, North Dakota, and Canada.* Self-published, Eagle Point, Ore.: 1993.

Howard, Joseph Kinsey. *Montana: High, Wide, and Handsome.* Yale University Press. New Haven: 1943.

Stabio, Bruce. *Stoneville, Montana.* 2009.

Stuart. *Forty Years on the Frontier, op. cit.*

Toole, K. Ross. *Montana: An Uncommon Land.* University of Oklahoma Press. Norman: 1959.

Brooks Brothers. https://en.wikipedia.org/wiki/Brooks_Brothers

Dupont. https://en.wikipedia.org/wiki/DuPont

Bugenstein, Michael D. *Map of Missouri River Wood Yards and Other Pertinent Sites, c.1884.* ©2019.

Annual Reports of the Board of Stock Commissioners and the Recorder of Marks and Brands, for the year 1892. Independent Publishing Co. Helena: 1893.

Cram, George F. *Map of Montana.* Chicago: 1890. University of Alabama Historical Map Archive. cartweb .geography.ua.edu/

Map of the Missouri River, From Its Mouth to Three Forks, Montana, Sheets 63-75. Missouri River Commission, 1893.

The Black Hills Journal. Rapid City, D.T. Feb. 15, 1884. www.newspapers.com

Black Hills Daily Pioneer. Deadwood, D.T. Feb. 19-20; 24, 1884. www.newspapers.com

Black Hills Daily Times. Deadwood, D.T. Feb. 16;19-20; Apr. 1, 1884. www.newspapers.com

Daily Yellowstone Journal, Miles City, M.T. Feb. 28; Nov. 20, 29, 1884. www.newspapers.com

The Yellowstone Journal, Miles City, Montana, July 21, 1883; Mar. 1, 1884. www.newspapers.com

Bismarck Weekly Tribune, June 27, 1884. www.newspapers.com

Sun River Sun, Sun River, M.T., Various issues, Sept. 21- Dec. 11, 1884. www.newspapers.com

River Press, op. cit., various issues, June 27-Aug., 1884, also July 20, 1892. www.montananewspapers.org./

Mineral Argus, Maiden, M.T. Various issues, July-Sept., 1884. www.newspapers.com

Glendive Times, Glendive, M.T. Various issues, Aug.-Nov., 1884. (microfilm)

Rocky Mountain Husbandman, White Sulphur Springs, M.T. Various issues, Aug.-Sept. 1884. www.newspapers.com

Carbon County Journal, Rawlins, Wyom. Terr. March 1, 1884; Apr. 24, 1886; July 27, 1889. Wyoming Newspaper Project www.pluto.wyo.gov

Bessemer Journal, Bessemer, Wyom. Terr. Aug. 1, 1889. Wyoming Newspaper Project. www.pluto.wyo.gov

The Buffalo Bulletin, Oct. 16, 1890. Wyoming Newspaper Project. www.pluto.wyo.gov

The Newcastle Journal, Newcastle, Wyo. June 19, 26; July 3, 1891. Wyoming Newspaper Project. www.pluto.wyo.gov

Weekly Tribune, Great Falls, Mont. July 30, 1892. www.newspapers.com

Red Lodge Picket, July 22 and Sept. 1893. www.newspapers.com

Valley County Gazette, Glasgow, Montana, Nov. 5, 1898. (From microfilm.)

Chapter 6

50 Years in the Saddle: Looking Back Down the Trail- Volume 4. © 1991. Manfred Signaless. Quality Quick Print, Dickinson, N.D.: 1991, and Image Printing, Bismarck, N.D.: 1991.

Board of Stock Commissioners. *Annual Report of the Recorder of Marks and Brands for the State of Montana for the Year 1892.* Independent Publishing Co. Helena: 1893.

Bismarck Daily Tribune, Bismarck, N.D. Apr. 8-9, 20; May 8; July 10, 1901. www.newspapers.com

Billings Gazette, Billings, Mont. Apr. 9; July 9, 1901. https://chroniclingamerica.loc.gov/

The Indianapolis Journal, Indianapolis, Ind. Apr. 8, 1901. www.newspapers.com

The St. Paul Globe, St Paul, Minn. Apr. 8, 1901. www.newspapers.com

Williston Graphic, Williston, N.D. Apr. 11, 1901. https://chroniclingamerica.loc.gov/

Dupuyer Acantha, Dupuyer, Mont. Apr. 11, 1901. https://chroniclingamerica.loc.gov/

Rosebud County News, Forsyth, Mont. Apr. 11, 1901. https://chroniclingamerica.loc.gov/

The Dickinson Press, Dickinson, N.D. Apr. 13; Apr. 27; May 18-25; Sept. 14, 1901. https://chroniclingamerica.loc.gov/

Glendive Independent, Glendive. Mont. Apr. 13, 1901. Original issue.

The Washburn Leader, Washburn, N.D. Apr. 13, 1901. www.newspapers.com

Morning World-Herald, Omaha, Neb. July 9, 1901. www.genealogybank.com

Chapter 7

Bugenstein, Michael D. *Since the Days of the Buffalo: A History of Eastern Montana and the Kalfell Ranch.* Published by Kalfell Ranch, Inc. Far Country Press. Helena: 2013.

Chaney, Roberta Carkeek. *Names on the Face of Montana.* Mountain Press Publishing Co., Missoula, Mont.: 1983.

Howard, Joseph Kinsey. *Montana: High Wide, and Handsome, op. cit.*

Sloan, Jim. *Nevada: True Tales from the Neon Wilderness.* University of Utah Press. Salt Lake City: 1993.

McCleary, Carrie. "Of Horses and Men: Superintendent Asbury's Deadly Assault on the Crow." *Tribal College Journal*, Vol. 14, No. 3- Spring 2003. (Provided by C. Adrian Heidenreich.)

Nabokov, Peter. *Two Leggings. . .* cited in Chapter 3. (Provided by C. Adrian Heidenreich.)

Oral conversations with Lance Kalfell concerning abandoned horses and range law, March-April, 2019.

Velma Bronn Johnston. https://en.wikipedia.org/wiki/Velma_Bronn_Johnston

Wild and Free-Roaming Horses and Burros Act of 1971. https://en.wikipedia.org/wiki/Wild_and_Free_Roaming_Horses_and_Burros_Act_of_1971

Pioche Weekly Record, Pioche, Nev., Jan 10, 1891. www.chroniclingamerica.loc.gov

Iron County News, Cedar City, Utah, Jan. 24, 1891. www.newspapers.com

Eureka Weekly Sentinel, Eureka, Nev., Feb 27, 1892. www.chroniclingamerica.loc.gov/

Lyon County Times, Dayton, Nev., Apr. 28, 1894. www.chroniclingamerica.loc.gov/
Salt Lake Herald, Salt Lake City, Utah, Nov. 21, 1894. www.chroniclingamerica.loc.gov/
Elko Independent, Elko, Nev., May 2, 1897. www.chroniclingamerica.loc.gov/
Yellowstone Monitor, Glendive, Mont., Aug. 13, 1908. www.newspapers.com
River Press, Fort Benton, Mont, June 2, 1909; Jan. 24, 1912. www.chroniclimgamerica.loc.gov
The Enterprise, Malta, Mont., May 15, 1913. www.chroniclingamerica.loc.gov/
The *Havre Daily News-Promoter,* Havre., Mont., June 4, 1926; Dec. 7, 1926. www.newspapers.com
Powder River Examiner and Broadus Independent, August 24, 1928. www.montanananewspapers.org/
The Ekalaka Eagle May 23, 1930. www.montananewspapers.org/
Reno Evening Gazette, Reno, Nev. Apr. 30, 1931; June 9, 1932; Nov. 15, 1933; Dec 22, 1936; March 29, 1938.
    www.newspapers.com

Appendix A

50 Years in the Saddle: Another Look at the Trail, Vol. 2. Published by Andrew Johnston, Dickinson, N. Dak.: The
    Story of J.M. (Mac) Uhlman, by Eugene B. Uhlman; The Stroud Brothers, by Andrew Johnston; The Reyn-
    olds Brothers, by Andrew Johnston; Jay Grantier, Taken from the *Watford City Guide,* Jan. 26, 1939. San
    Felipe Press, Austin, Tex.: 1963.
Bugenstein, *Since the Days of the Buffalo, op. cit.*
Many, many oral interviews with Arnold Ceynar, descendant of Mac Uhlman of the Bird Head Ranch.
Original brand registration for Morning Star Cattle Company, State of North Dakota livestock record, May 11,
    1893.
Brands and Marks of the Members of the North Dakota Stock Growers' Association: 1892. Pioneer Publishing Co.
    Mandan, N.D.: 1892. (Original in Princeton University.) Digitized by Google. https://babel.hathitrust.org/
Van Dersal's Directory of Marks and Brands for the State of North Dakota. Sam'l Van Dersal, Publisher, Bismarck,
    N.D. McGill-Warner Co. Printers. St. Paul, Minn.: 1902. https://books.google.com
Van Deral and Connor's Stockgrowers' Directory of Marks and Brands for the State of Montana 1872-1900. Helena:
    1900. Reprinted by Review Publishing Co. Glendive, Mont.: 1976.
Brand Book of the Montana Stockgrowers' Association for 1903. Independent Publishing Co. Helena, Mont.: 1903.
Map of the Missouri River, op. cit. Sheets 49-59.
Yellowstone Journal, Sept. 30, 1882. www.newspapers.com
Live Stock Reporter, Miles City, Mont., July 4, 1891. (Microfilm.)
Yellowstone Journal, July – 1892. (Microfilm.)
 River Press, July 12, 1893; Aug. 29, 1894. (Original volumes.)
The Daily Courier, Connellsville, Pa. Dec. 6, 1911.

Appendix B

Bugenstein. *Since the Days of the Buffalo, op cit.*
Flatbed press (Printing). https://britannica.com/technology/flatbed-press
Linotype machine. https://en.wikipedia.org/wiki/Linotype_machine
Halftone. https://en.wikipedia.org/wiki/Halftone
River Press. Various issues, 1895. (From original volumes.)
Richland Beacon-News, Rayville, La., March 18, 1893. www.newspapers.com